Praise for *Bulletproof Spirit*

"Having suffered from post-traumatic stress as a police officer, I know what can happen when we are exposed to unthinkable traumas. This book and the wellness strategies it describes have helped to save my life."

— **police officer,** Davenport, Iowa

"In my twenty-five years as an officer and now part of command staff, this book and the training offered by Captain Willis are the most meaningful and useful I have ever experienced."

— **police captain,** Jefferson Parish, Louisiana

"Clear, compassionate, and to the point, this guidebook is an excellent resource for the newest academy graduate and for the longtime veteran....Captain Willis conveys the importance of health, wellness, and departmental support, and he openly explains the hazards of the job and how to maintain career peak performance. This book is now a first choice for all the emergency first responders I work with."

— **Sara Gilman, MFT,** psychotherapist and president, Coherence Associates, Inc.

"Any police professional with a serious commitment to understanding and mitigating the professional and personal stresses of a police career knows well the names Violanti, Kirschman, Gilmartin, and Grossman. The name of Captain Dan Willis can now be added to this respected list of leaders in police-officer health and wellness. In *Bulletproof Spirit*, Captain Willis successfully combines aspects of science, spirituality, and his personal experience to provide pragmatic approaches for individual officers and police organizations to maximize their health and lon-gevity in their police careers. If you challenges of stress in your life and career (and all officers are), *Bulletproof Spirit* is an important and useful read."

— **Michael J. Asken, PhD,** police performance psychologist, author of *MindSighting: Mental Toughness Skills for Police Officers in High Stress Situations*

"Written from the heart (and from the trenches), the book is direct, passionate, and insightful. Willis discusses the role of faith in service, peer and family support, the basics of wellness protocols, and treating stress disorders."

— **Anna Jedrziewski,** *Retailing Insight*

"After over thirty years in law enforcement, I have witnessed far too many times the emotional damage a career as a first responder can have. *Bulletproof Spirit* details practical steps that are not only effective but essential to help protect and ensure the wellness of those who serve. This book is a must-read for all first responders and their families — the wellness and emotional survival of these heroes depends upon it, as well as the safety of our communities."

— **Shelley Zimmerman,** Chief of Police (ret.), San Diego Police Department

"This is not just a report from a top-notch expert on psychology, or a well-done how-to book by a more-than-competent writer, or even a thoughtful motivational book that will undoubtedly bring you new spiritual inspiration. It is actually all three of these books between two covers, written by a police captain who has earned his credibility in the day-to-day work of being a law-enforcement officer and first responder for many years — a man who has worked the streets and also managed from the top down.... The book tells you why you might be traumatized by any number of criminal or emergency situations, and it offers case studies of events that would be hard to live with in the minds of even the strongest personalities. And then it brings suggestions, guidelines, and resolutions to help us live with the problems, crises, and destructions which we see every day in the lives of others. *Trauma intervention* is a term we have all come to know, and Dan Willis convinces us why we should take that term seriously, instructing us on how to bring peace to ourselves and our families after living through chaos."

— **Dennis Smith**,
author of *Report from Ground Zero*

"If there was ever a time in history when we needed the answers to address critical emotional-survival issues of our emergency first responders, it is now! Issues of saving marriages, careers, and lives within our emergency-first-responder professions are everyone's responsibility within our ranks. A great first step would be to read and immediately put into practice Captain Dan Willis's recommendations in *Bulletproof Spirit*."

— **Robert Douglas Jr.**, executive director (ret.),
National Police Suicide Foundation

"Captain Willis has written a practical, extremely useful, and important guide for first responders everywhere. *Bulletproof Spirit* is a vital resource for every first responder, caregiver, and agency manager. This book offers the essential keys for preparation for, protection from, and healing after trauma for all those devoted to public safety."

— **Catherine Butler, PhD, EdD, MFT**,
psychologist to emergency first responders

"As I read *Bulletproof Spirit*, I found it difficult to put down. Captain Willis presents the truth that 'it's all right for the helper to ask for help' in a manner that proves to be thought-provoking and highly informative. He utilizes real-life stories from the warriors who have walked through the valley. His work emphasizes the significance of wellness encompassing the mind, body, and spirit, and he reminds us that it is vital not only to nurture but to be nurtured as well. Be prepared to honestly look at your-self in the mirror and determine if you possess a 'bulletproof soul.'"

— **Bobby Smith, PhD**, former Louisiana State Trooper
and author of *Visions of Courage* and *The Will to Survive*

"First responders typically do not understand the potentially dev-astating extent of the impact their chosen professions can have upon their minds, bodies, spirits, health, and families. *Bullet-proof Spirit* provides an essential and practical guide for all those who enable them to live and serve in health and wellness."

— **Nancy Bohl-Penrod, PhD**, founder of the Counseling Team
International and expert on first-responder trauma

"*Bulletproof Spirit* exposes the silent dangers, and sometimes killers, of many of our first-responder heroes in a dynamic and compassionate way. . . . Read this book and think about the good people who wear the badge and the terribly inhumane things they experience. *Bulletproof Spirit* will help heal first responders and help them find purpose and happiness once again. It is an honor to endorse this book. It *will* save lives."

— **Clarke Paris**, Las Vegas Metro police sergeant (ret.),
author of *My Life for Your Life*, president of
The Pain Behind the Badge Training LLC

"This book would be a valuable asset to any first responder, cli-nician, or peer-support person working with first responders."

— **Kevin Gilmartin, PhD**, author of
Emotional Survival for Law Enforcement

BULLETPROOF SPIRIT

BULLETPROOF SPIRIT

REVISED EDITION

The First Responder's Essential Resource for Protecting and Healing Mind and Heart

CAPTAIN DAN WILLIS
La Mesa Police Department (ret.)

FOREWORD BY DONALD BOSTIC

New World Library
Novato, California

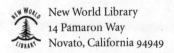

New World Library
14 Pamaron Way
Novato, California 94949

Grateful acknowledgment is made to Julia Holladay for permission to include the results of her study in conjunction with San Diego Police Department.

Text design by Tona Pearce Myers

The Library of Congress has cataloged the original edition as follows:
Willis, Dan, date.
Bulletproof spirit : the first responder's essential resource for protecting and healing mind and heart / Dan Willis, Captain, La Mesa Police Department.
     pages   cm
Includes bibliographical references and index.
ISBN 978-1-60868-261-4 (paperback) — ISBN 978-1-60868-262-1 (ebook)
1. Stress management. 2. Self-help. 3. Job stress. 4. First responders. I. Title.
RA785.W533 2014
155.9—dc23   2014015736

First printing of revised edition, August 2019
ISBN 978-1-60868-631-5
Ebook ISBN 978-1-60868-632-2
Printed in Canada on 100% postconsumer-waste recycled paper

10 9 8 7 6

We shall draw from the heart of suffering itself
the means of inspiration and survival.

— WINSTON CHURCHILL

CONTENTS

FOREWORD

by Donald Bostic

Supervisory Special Agent (SSA) Donald Bostic is an instructor in the Executive Programs Instruction Unit at the Federal Bureau of Investigation (FBI) National Academy at Quantico, Virginia. Specializing in topics related to officer wellness, SSA Bostic instructs police executives from around the world. This foreword is the opinion of SSA Bostic and does not reflect an official endorsement by the FBI.

In my current role as a Supervisory Special Agent for the FBI, instructing police managers from throughout the United States and all over the world, I have found *Bulletproof Spirit* to be an invaluable resource — a career-survival manual — for any first responder. I use it as required reading in my wellness courses at the FBI National Academy in Quantico, Virginia. Officers routinely report back to me how useful and meaningful they have found the many practical wellness strategies so clearly explained in this emotional-survival resource.

Captain Dan Willis learned early in his police career how essential it was for him to find ways to heal and to prevent becoming crippled by the many traumas of a first-responder career. As first responders, we are practically useless to others if we are suffering within. This wellness guidebook teaches you how to maintain your motivation, health, and wellness in order to protect, serve, and give life to others. As Captain Willis describes, a career of professional service can suffocate your heart and cause many debilitating effects in your personal and professional life. He shows you how to remain driven by your heart to serve with purposeful compassion to make a positive difference and, in so doing, to activate the heart's tremendous capacity to heal from trauma in order to help protect and serve others.

One day, while flying to one of my teaching engagements on first-responder wellness, I realized this invaluable lesson of taking care of yourself *before* you are able to care for anyone else. My carry-on luggage was crammed in the overhead compartment, and my freshly laundered sport coat that had been neatly folded and placed on top of it was now crumpled under another passenger's dirty backpack. The delayed, overbooked flight was causing me much stress and anxiety. I found myself becoming more frustrated and angrier as my seat was changed from the usually requested aisle seat to a middle seat between two equally stressed travelers.

The flight attendant's voice droned on with the typical pre-flight instructions that I, like most other passengers, ignored because I had heard them numerous times before. However, in an unexpected moment of focus on her voice, I recognized the often-repeated instructions, "If you are traveling with a child or someone who requires assistance, secure your mask first, and then assist the other person." I'd never really thought much about this safety instruction before. But as I sat there trying to get comfortable, these words echoed with deep meaning in my mind.

Thirty-two years as a state and federal law-enforcement officer, EMT, employee assistance peer counselor, and church leader/volunteer have clearly defined me as someone who loves to serve and help others. Late nights, holidays, and many long hours away from my family have been spent helping others in their times of need. Domestic disturbances, fatal car crashes, drug overdoses, violent crime scenes, suicides and other senseless deaths, overseas trips to war zones, and many natural disasters all have been "horrible opportunities" to help victims, witnesses, and, at times, other officers.

I was always instinctively careful to first place *their* "oxygen masks" on as quickly and securely as possible in order to give them the care, safety, and compassion that they needed and expected. But what about my "oxygen mask"? What was I doing to ensure that I was taking care of myself in order to be able to be a strong, healthy, caring first responder who could save and influence others' lives? Years of committed service to others had left me emotionally, mentally, physically, and spiritually exhausted and out of breath; depleted, I had become quite limited in my ability to serve others while remaining engaged, compassionate, healthy, and resilient.

The distractions surrounding me on the flight were hindering my ability to focus on the safety instructions. The repetitive verbal instructions of flight attendant after flight attendant seemed to take on less importance to me. So, too, had I disregarded the many warning signs in my life of service that should have alerted me to the crippling effects of trauma. "I am okay; I can handle it; it's part of the job" became robotic responses to what should have been opportunities to self-reflect about my own health.

Over time I came to realize that I was not alone. Thousands upon thousands of committed public servants strive every day to make sure our communities are safe and the countless needs of the public are met. Very often this is accomplished at tremendous personal cost. Firefighters, police officers, EMTs, and military personnel train to give their best effort to others, but who is helping the helpers? It is critical for the safety of our communities and for the survival of those who serve them that we must recognize the seriousness of this issue and make the necessary changes to ensure that first responders are healthy and well in all aspects of their lives. *Bulletproof Spirit* is a necessary and vital first step toward this end.

Bulletproof Spirit is an outstanding resource that is essential to first responders as well as to friends and family members who care deeply about them. Captain Willis has written this career-survival manual in a way that gives practical and insightful guidance to help first responders "put on their oxygen masks before assisting others." He gives thoughtful consideration to the needed balance, training, and enhancement of physical, emotional, mental, and spiritual wellness in the lives of first responders. His unique experiences in his thirty-year law-enforcement career and as a graduate of the FBI National Academy allow him to write with the authority of someone who has "been there" and with the compassion and insight of a teacher driven to help prevent first-responder suicides and to save not only careers, but lives. He does not offer academic theories or faceless statistics to support his observations; instead, readers will naturally see themselves in the true-life stories provided and will most assuredly feel the powerful hope and positive message that come with his many useful and practical instructions on developing and maintaining a "bulletproof spirit."

In the fall of 2018, I invited Captain Willis to return to the FBI National Academy to speak to his peers about his journey beyond mere survival toward peace, health, and wellness. He eloquently shared how his experience as a student at the Academy had ignited his interest in the topic of officer wellness and initiated his quest to write this book. Police executives who attend the ten-week course at Quantico, Virginia, are removed from the everyday distractions and demands of work at their departments and are able to focus on themselves and the changes they want to make when they return home. Reflections on their own wellness and the wellness of those they supervise have revealed life-changing observations to many students.

After reading *Bulletproof Spirit*, officers from across the globe have told me how invaluable they have found this book. One officer recently commented that he was hesitant to say the book "saved his life," but he was certain the book "changed his life." The voluminous informational content of the book, as well as the clear manner in which it is written, has made it a priority choice for many first-responder agencies around the world to provide copies to their employees, both civilian and sworn, and include it in their resource libraries. This new, revised edition of *Bulletproof Spirit* promises to add even more value with updated information, two new chapters, and additional techniques to improve first-responder wellness.

Wellness and emotional survival are topics that demand ever-increasing attention in today's world of seemingly insurmountable challenges to first responders. Regardless of the career stage you find yourself in now, this book will likely prove critically helpful to increasing your survivability, health, and wellness throughout your entire career and beyond.

Having this information at the beginning of a career can help ensure a long, productive life of service and prevent you from suffering much heartache. Getting this invaluable information midcareer can help get a first responder back on the right track to balanced wellness, peace, motivation, and resiliency, and restore the great satisfaction they once felt in serving others. Understanding this information as an executive leader of first responders will allow you to identify dangerous signs and symptoms of the effects of trauma and will equip you to create and implement wellness policies, procedures, and programs that make your organization healthier, more effective, more efficient, and more professional in its service to the community. If you love someone who is a first responder, this information will assist you in understanding their struggles and empower you to "help a helper." It can help save your marriage, their career, and their life.

Relax, read the book, and enjoy your flight!

PREFACE

As a first responder, if you are not driven by your heart to make a positive difference with every call, with your colleagues, within your agency, and within the community, then the job is likely going to eat you alive. Prolonged exposure to violence, trauma, death, and suffering can scar a first responder's spirit and take a terrible toll; substance abuse, depression, post-traumatic stress disorder, emotional suffering, suicide, and lost careers plague these honored professions. The effects of the invisible wounds of the job ripple outward, and the wear and tear affect not just the first responders themselves but also their friends, family, colleagues, and the community they are devoted to protecting. Their spirits can suffer a death by a thousand cuts, each traumatic incident causing the soul to bleed a little more. The lack of sufficient wellness training and training in emotional survival for these emergency first responders has become a critical issue for all of us.

How has the job affected you? How have you changed over the years? How has the job affected your sleep, your health, your relationships, your home life? How has it affected your view of people and the overall quality of your life?

Losing a first responder to emotional and psychological trauma should never be a side effect of the job. There are proven, effective methods that enhance resiliency, heal, and inspire. These wellness strategies, in a sense, "bulletproof" the first responder's spirit. This book offers essential principles for emotional survival — and hope.

Early in my police career, I recognized the critical need for training in emotional survival and realized that the job was slowly poisoning my spirit. This sudden realization came while I was celebrating my stepdaughter's eighth birthday with a party at the house. Children of all ages raced around our yard, laughing and screaming over the music blasting from outside speakers. My wife supervised the bouncy house while one of our neighbors manned the grill, turning out dozens of hot dogs and hamburgers for the partygoers. An elaborate pink princess cake topped with eight candles sat in the very center of a picnic table, next to a stack of gifts.

Everyone in attendance appeared to be having a wonderful time, except for me. I sat in a lawn chair watching the festivities with what I knew must be a cold, distant look in my eyes. I was surrounded by family and longtime friends, many of them fellow officers. Yet I did not feel like part of the scene or connected to anyone. I wasn't happy or sad, just indifferent to everything and everyone. I didn't want or feel much of anything and hadn't for quite some time. I simply didn't care about anything anymore. Inside, I felt nothing at all.

I smiled and cheered along with the others as I watched my stepdaughter make a wish, blow out the candles on her cake, and open her presents; but the gestures were empty. And then it hit me: I had seen this cold distance before in many of my colleagues during my seven years on the job. I knew where this road led, and it was never somewhere good. I had achieved my life's dream when I became a police officer. From day one, I'd put my whole heart and soul into my work. When had I started to lose my spirit? I had become someone my loved ones no longer recognized, someone I did not recognize. Would I become another casualty of the job?

From the time I was just a kid I wanted a job where I could make a difference and positively affect people's lives. I wanted to help people, every single day. I wanted to protect life and serve others. In high school, I set my sights on becoming a police officer.

After graduating from San Diego State with a criminal justice degree, I was hired by the La Mesa Police Department, and I loved it. After three years I became a detective. The idea of hunting down those who perpetuate evil and cause so much suffering, and bringing them to justice, gave my life purpose. Every time a criminal was put behind bars, I had the satisfaction of knowing that I had removed a dangerous threat and was saving dozens of people from being victimized.

I could not have been more passionate about the work and the job. But a steady barrage of senseless violence slowly, inexorably began to take its toll. The nature of police work was depleting my spirit. The innocent kid who once dreamed of becoming a police officer had turned into a hardened and emotionally numb adult. I had become emotionally dead inside, distant from others, disengaged, disinterested, and progressively more uncaring. I learned firsthand just how insidious the adverse effects of the job could be as I continued to be changed in several ways by the job. I felt helpless to stop what was happening; I had no training in how to survive emotionally and maintain wellness. Every day, I slipped a bit further into a fate that is far too common for first responders.

Throughout my career I've watched as tragedies involved first-responder colleagues. Police departments and other first-responder agencies hire good people, which makes it even more disturbing when officers turn bad, self-destruct, and even kill themselves. What causes a police officer to become dishonest or a thief, or to sexually assault somebody on duty? What makes them throw away their family and career to drink themselves nearly to death? Or stick their own gun in their mouth to end their suffering? These men and women weren't hired because they demonstrated criminal or self-destructive tendencies; it was just the opposite. Tragically, what they experience while doing the job can cause irreparable harm to their spirits. Without proper emotional-survival training, the first responder's job can destroy lives.

None of these heroes who sacrifice a part of themselves for others go from loving their job to waking up one day helplessly lost. It's a slow and gradual process, one I wasn't even aware was happening to me until that moment at the birthday party. The realization that I could no longer feel hit me like a thunderbolt. That was just the first of many hard realizations. I also had to acknowledge that solving the murder case that had been all-consuming for the preceding four years really wasn't the answer to everything. I had lost touch with my family and with all the other things that brought balance and sustenance to my life. I'd spent too much time hunting predators and suffering with my victims. It had been months since I'd done the things I loved, like hiking or swimming in the ocean. What it all added up to was that I had lost my inner self and my spirit was suffering.

It was time to take positive action to pull myself out of the hole before it was too late. I had to get back in touch with the things I loved, that made my spirit come alive. I needed to do all the things that tend to fall by the wayside once you become a first responder, or I would become a victim of my beloved profession. And make no mistake about it: being a first responder is not your typical job. You have to make an exhaustive and consistent effort to keep the job from overwhelming you. The biggest lesson I learned was that the job was suffocating my heart. I realized that any first-responder job is truly a vocation of the heart, and if you're not putting your heart into your work by trying to make a difference, then the job can slowly destroy you.

I desperately didn't want to end up like other officers I had seen, some of whose stories you will read in this book. I would eventually become no good to anyone if I didn't learn how to protect my spirit and survive emotionally. There are so many walking-wounded colleagues out there, desperately needing help and slogging along with post-traumatic stress disorder (PTSD) or major depression, struggling to make it through each day, helpless and hopeless, feeling they can't ask for help. They become more and more miserable, cynical, negative, and bitter, while thinking everyone else is a criminal. Somehow, over the years, they have lost all connection with their spouses and kids, who seem like strangers. Worst of all, they truly believe that no one understands them, and so they lose hope.

There are practical, effective methods to help first responders survive emotionally and to heal their spirits. It is no longer inevitable that these careers will lead to broken lives and irreparable harm. There is absolutely no reason why police officers, as well as firefighters, career military officers, and all other first responders, cannot thrive and be well throughout their careers and retire from a lifetime of noble service with a vibrant mind, body, and spirit. They deserve to enjoy their careers and the rest of their lives in peace, happiness, and good health. They should be able to look back on their careers with pride while looking forward to savoring all the good that's still to come.

I served as a police officer for nearly thirty years. And today I bring the passion and excitement I have always had for my work and am channeling it toward the critical cause of promoting emotional wellness for first responders. The hazards of the first-responder professions are so many: drugs, alcohol, gambling, depression, PTSD, suicide, emotional illness, broken families. And the resulting harm throughout our communities is a tragic, preventable waste and a shame.

To me there are no better, more fulfilling, or more honorable jobs than those of first responders, for they protect and give life to others. The sacrifices and work of emergency first responders are the only things preventing our society from becoming overrun with evil, cruelty, and oppression. It is essential for first responders to learn how to bulletproof their spirits so that they can most effectively protect the rest of us.

INTRODUCTION

When we are no longer able to change a situation,
we are challenged to change ourselves.

— Viktor E. Frankl

The safety of our communities is inherently connected to the health and wellness of the first responders serving them. Every first-responder agency needs to provide the most professional, ethical, and effective services, while every first responder needs to serve without suffering from trauma, post-traumatic stress, low resiliency, addictions, depression, or low motivation. This is a career-survival manual, a wellness and emotional-survival guidebook that offers a blueprint for a healthy, motivated, resilient, and professional first responder.

The diminished health and wellness of first responders is extremely disheartening. The number one cause of death for police officers is suicide — there are nearly 200 such deaths every year in the United States (on average about 120 to 140 documented yearly, with unknown additional deaths improperly classified as "accidental" or "undetermined"). The rate of suicides for retired police increases tenfold. Military statistics are even grimmer. On average, one active-duty soldier and 21 veterans commit suicide every day. Of all working police officers, 15 to 18 percent (about 120,000) have post-traumatic stress disorder, while over 200,000 vets suffer from this disorder. Suicide and depression have also become a serious concern for those in the fire service, corrections officers, public-safety dispatchers, and EMTs (emergency medical technicians), with some estimates showing PTSD rates of nearly 30 percent.

It is estimated that 25 to 30 percent of police officers have stress-based physical health problems, such as high blood pressure, heart ailments, circulatory disorders, digestive disorders, diabetes, certain kinds of cancer, and premature aging. Stress can also cause significant sleep disorders, fatigue, isolation, irritability, anger, intrusive thoughts, depression, anxiety, paranoia, and panic reactions. A 2007 research study by Harvard Medical School, published in the *Journal of the American Medical Association*, reports that 40 percent of police officers have a serious sleeping disorder that causes significant health problems. Acute stress is a major factor in early retirement and career changes for first responders, causing the public to lose the service of many solid, experienced men and women. In my experience, about 50 percent of police officers and many other first responders retire early or leave on disability.

My Own Experience

I still get nauseated remembering the seven hundred photos on a child molester's computer depicting infants and small children being forcibly sodomized and forced to perform other sex acts. As much as I would like to forget them, those images will be seared into my mind forever, as will the details of the case where a janitor at an Alzheimer's facility brutally raped an eighty-year-old invalid patient.

Several of my fellow officers have fought hand to hand for their lives; some very nearly became murder victims. Others were left with no choice but to kill another in order to save a life, or became the unwitting instrument of death in a suicide-by-cop. Try, if you will, for just a minute to imagine watching a dying man take his last breath — a man who deliberately forced you to kill him because he couldn't take his own life.

Then there are the accidents, like the one where a young woman was trapped in her vehicle after a crash. She was incinerated right before the eyes of horrified officers at the scene, who frantically tried, and failed, to rescue her. The woman's screams became more and more anguished until they abruptly stopped. The officers could do nothing but stand helplessly by, feeling the searing heat burn their own skin as the unforgettable stench of burning flesh washed over them. How do you forget a scene like that? How do you go home and be normal?

As a police officer I have walked into homes of such poverty and deplorable filth that I was unable to eat from disgust. Such was the case after seeing a small boy covered in cockroach feces lying in a bed covered in his own filth. My partner and I quickly hustled him out of there, only to learn two days later that the social services agency had returned that child to live in the same home.

We have witnessed crime scenes of unimaginable horror: The kitchen of a small house where a butchered mother lay murdered on the floor, and a set of tiny, bloody footprints led to the rear of the house. There officers discovered a four-year-old girl curled up on her bed in the fetal position. She had been stabbed to death.

The body of a woman who came home early and surprised an intruder, who proceeded to stab her seventy-six times, finally breaking the knife blade off in her skull. Or the body of the man who was slashed repeatedly with a sword; officers found his body lying in his living room with his intestines sprawled several feet in various directions all over the floor.

I have crawled on my hands and knees inside a body bag to search for and collect maggots so I could give them to an entomologist to approximate the time of death of a murder victim. I have chased armed robbery suspects at 120 miles an hour, eventually catching them. I have been involved in numerous fights, had my life threatened several times, been shot at, and had my police car's rear window shot out. I have observed numerous autopsies, each time getting covered in a fine mist of skull dust when the medical examiner used a high-powered saw to cut through a skull to remove a brain. I've even posed as an inmate in jail to try to get a murder suspect to talk about his shooting.

I worked exhaustively to bring a child molester to justice twenty-seven years after he committed his crimes — at the time, the longest period between a crime and conviction in San Diego County history. I spent four years investigating a murder, even though the victim's body was never found, and won one of the first no-body murder convictions in San Diego County.

As my years on the force went by, the dead and decomposing bodies became too numerous to mention. I saw the many different ways that people kill themselves; the unspeakable damage criminals inflict upon children; the broken bodies resulting from scenes of senseless gang-related or domestic violence; the mangled corpses of accident scenes. Each and every one of these scenes traumatized me in various ways, including suffocating my heart, which no doubt contributed to the failure of two marriages. Still, I persevered while my spirit suffered.

The Breaking Point

Thinking of the James Desmond case immediately brings on a feeling of horror like no other. Every detail is clear in my mind as I once again stand over the lifeless remains of a body discovered lying in an obscure alley, minus its head and hands. These appendages had been savagely sawed off with some sort of manual tree-trimming saw and discarded elsewhere, never to be found. As I stood over the partial corpse of what until very recently had been a living, breathing man, I wondered yet again what kind of sociopath could do something this horrible to another human being.

Movies and computer games have accustomed general audiences to scenes of shocking violence, and CGI (computer-generated imagery) effects have become more and more realistic. However, nothing can come close to the real-life grisly sight of a bright-red open torso where a head was very recently attached. I wondered about the fear the victim must have felt just before his murder and shuddered to imagine his agony. My spirit suffered a tremendous blow working over such a grotesque scene — a scene that will never leave my mind.

That day marked the beginning of seven years of emotionally exhausting and frustrating work on this most difficult case. We ascertained that the victim had been a middle-aged man named James Desmond. There was no known crime scene — he had been killed and cut up at another, unknown location. There were no known witnesses, no confessions, no cause of death, no murder weapon, and no DNA — no fingerprints, hair, or other trace evidence of the killer left at the scene. In fact, there was no physical evidence of any kind left by the killer. Still, I refused to let such a heinous murder go unpunished. For the next seven years I didn't work the case; I lived it. Living the case meant immersing myself in an underworld of gangs, prostitutes, pimps, and drug dealers.

I gradually became a different person while working the Desmond murder. My perspective on life and the way in which I viewed other people and the world at large changed significantly for the worse. My suspicion and distrust of people, even family members, grew exponentially as I endured death threats and was followed home by an accomplice of the suspects. I was constantly looking over my shoulder. I became emotionally distant from my wife and stepkids as I obsessed over every detail of the case, wanting to try anything and everything in my power to solve it before the murderers killed again. Losing myself in such a dark world was consuming my very spirit.

I did not work in vain. Seven years after we discovered the body in an alley, two members of the Los Angeles Crips gang were convicted of the murder of James Desmond. I had done what I had promised his family I would do. However, I was no longer the person who had stood over his mangled corpse in horror. I was in real danger of becoming another victim of my profession, brought down by the accumulation of too many haunting experiences. I was having serious difficulty sleeping, I felt emotionless, and I was becoming increasingly more isolated and distant and less and less able to cope with stress. I realized that I had to develop my own emotional- and spiritual-survival practices or I would not survive.

I take the "protect and serve" aspects of the first responder's job as sacrosanct. It is our sacred duty to protect life and provide help when people need it. It is our responsibility to maintain emotional, mental, physical, and spiritual wellness in order to be there for those who need and depend on us. Our fellow citizens deserve nothing less than a dedicated, healthy, and complete first responder who is emotionally stable, fully invested in the job, and willing and able to do everything in his or her power to serve those in need. It is my great hope that this book will give you the proven, effective tools to be your very best: a hero who enables the rest of us to live a safe and secure life.

Initially, it is important for you to realize that to cultivate and sustain wellness, all the components of a person must be addressed: mind, body, emotions, and, most important, spirit. It is your responsibility to use the information in this book to develop your own emotional-survival and wellness practices based on the initiatives described.

In this book I share what I learned in my nearly thirty years on the job and from my own personal trials. I offer practical, effective solutions and proactive wellness initiatives that have worked to heal and protect my spirit and the spirits of many others. The essential survival principles, beginning with the warning signs and self-awareness discussed in chapter 1, offer a practical resource guide to all first responders who seek to bulletproof their spirits. Chapter 2 explains many ways to nurture, sustain, and shield your spirit while enhancing resiliency, motivation, and wellness. Chapter 4 highlights an officer's experience of trauma and post-traumatic stress disorder, and his process of healing, while chapter 5 offers several survival lessons of other first responders. Chapter 6 discusses the spirituality of service and how compassion and life-affirming acts can strengthen resiliency and heal your spirit. Methods to mitigate the hypervigilance cycle and to prepare for and allay the effects of acute stress and trauma are described in chapters 3 and 7. The many benefits of the BeSTOW (Beyond Survival Toward Officer Wellness) philosophy are listed in chapter 8; peer-support concepts are discussed in chapter 9; and the many ways your loved ones can support you are described in chapter 10. Chapter 11 tells of the essential ways a chaplain can heal and sustain your spirit. All of this information is vital. It was vital for Officer Tim Purdy, as you will read in chapter 12, and he credits it with saving his career and even his life.

Chapter One

THE WARNING SIGNS AND SELF-AWARENESS

He who has health, has hope;
and he who has hope, has everything.
— Thomas Carlyle

La Mesa, 1986. It's the end of another busy three-till-eleven-PM police shift punctuated by numerous calls from all over the city, requiring endless accompanying reports. Officer Troy wants nothing more than to go home and fall into bed. With just five minutes left till he clocks out, he drives toward the city gas pumps to refuel his police car. The area is isolated at this time of night, the few surrounding businesses closed and dark. He sees a car parked by itself in a dark alcove near an alley. In the faint yellow streetlight, he automatically notes that its windows are steamed up, making it impossible to see inside. Just some teenagers making out, he thinks, driving past. He will never know exactly why, but a nagging sense that something is out of place — that something is wrong — makes him stop, turn around, park, and approach the car on foot.

He shines his flashlight directly into the rear window on the driver's side, trying to see through the haze on the steamy glass. Squinting, he can barely make out a silver shimmer in the weak beam. His heart races as he realizes that the shimmer is a large knife blade — one being held to the throat of a partially nude woman. She is lying on her side in the back seat with her hands tied behind her back. He has stumbled upon a brutal rape.

Troy draws his handgun and yells at the man to drop the knife. His repeated orders are drowned out by the shrill screams of the victim. Her assailant jumps into the driver's seat and jams a key into the ignition. Troy tries frantically to pull the locked door open. Keeping his handgun pointed directly at the rapist's head, he uses his flashlight to pound against the driver's window in a futile attempt to shatter the glass. "Don't start the car or I'll shoot! Hands up in the air! Get out of the car now or I WILL SHOOT!"

The engine turns over, and as the car is slammed into drive, Troy knows he has no choice. He fires one shot directly into the man's left temple. The rapist slumps over as shattered glass and blood spatter the officer's face and uniform. Momentarily blinded, he wipes his face and then moves to try to assist the battered young woman in the back seat. She is completely hysterical, screaming and fighting and pushing him away as he tries to reassure her and assess her injuries. When backup arrives, with lights flashing and sirens screaming, Officer Troy looks like he's been through a war.

The entire confrontation lasted for less than thirty seconds. In thirty seconds Officer Troy saved one life and took another. The police academy never taught him just how life changing a few seconds on the job can be. As is the case for many first responders in life-threatening situations, these few seconds will adversely affect the rest of his life. From this night on, he will be plagued by sleepless nights, nightmares during the few hours he can sleep, and periodic anxiety attacks. In no time at all, Troy seemed to develop a classic case of (undiagnosed) post-traumatic stress disorder. His life will become defined by this one moment, and Troy will feel imprisoned by the helpless feeling of not knowing how to heal.

Officer Troy's spirit was vulnerable because he never had emotional-survival training. In contrast, an officer at an adjacent agency has been involved in seven shootings, five of them fatal. Although he experienced some difficult issues related to these shootings, he has fared far better because he has had training and learned wellness practices that prepared and protected his spirit.

I was a young police officer new on the job when Officer Troy's shooting occurred. The department reacted by conducting the required investigation but offered little in support and assistance to Troy, who inwardly was struggling. It was quickly established that the dead man had been released from prison just one week earlier and had abducted the young woman. The investigators ruled that the shooting was justified, and everyone just moved on.

Troy was cleared of any wrongdoing and, in fact, had done excellent work with his heroic action of saving a life. As soon as that was established, his fellow officers and superiors tended to act as though the shooting had never happened. No one meant to be uncaring or cruel by leaving Troy on his own to just get on with it; episodes such as this shooting were, unfortunately, part of the job, and it was thought best to try to simply move on as quickly as possible. Officer Troy did not know how to constructively process such a traumatic incident and put it into the proper perspective.

He was tormented by vivid images of that night and panic attacks that eventually became almost crippling. I watched Troy go from being a well-liked, friendly, and dynamic part of the force to becoming negative, bitter, and angry toward the police department. He would bad-mouth every directive, every new initiative from management, with contempt. His trauma experiences affected not only his work, but his personal life as well.

The superiors in my agency might have tried to prevent this kind of outcome, but what should they — and we, his fellow officers — have done? At that time no one in my police department had any knowledge of how to support and care for the spirit of an officer involved in such a critical incident. And the soul-poisoning incidents that the average emergency first responder witnesses over the course of a career are many and varied. As a rookie officer, I had no idea of the kind of evil I would witness over the next decades. I would eventually learn that the first step was to become aware of the warning signs in my behavior and to recognize how the job was affecting me and what I could proactively do to shield my spirit, work through trauma, and maintain wellness.

The First Component of Wellness: Understanding the Nine Warning Signs

There are numerous specific warning signs that should alert you, as an emergency first responder, and your family members to the fact that you are becoming a victim of your profession. These warning signs and associated problems never simply go away on their own. Instead, they progressively, insidiously, worsen over time if not corrected. You need to become self-aware, realize when you are displaying these danger signs, and then choose to proactively address the problem in a constructive way, before it becomes too late and the problem irreparably harms the quality of your personal and professional life.

Any one of these warning signs is a serious indication that you are having difficulty processing the acute stress and trauma of the job. These warning signs do not typically occur in a progression; any or all can occur if you have not worked to bulletproof your spirit.

1. Isolation

Over time there is a natural tendency, in all first-responder jobs, for the individual to become increasingly isolated. This involves withdrawing — preferring the company of work colleagues or being alone to associating with other friends, family, and their related activities. You develop the tendency to disengage, not wanting to make decisions away from work, and preferring not to be involved with others — even spouses and children. Eventually, you can become distant and reclusive. Close work bonds are desirable, but you need the counterbalance of other friends more than you need anyone else. Hanging out exclusively with first-responder colleagues tends to reinforce any negative aspects of the profession's worldview. "Outside" friends will help keep you from developing a victim mentality (feeling victimized by work, by society, the agency, and so on) and also from thinking everyone is a criminal. As we isolate ourselves, we increasingly become disconnected from others, uncaring, disengaged with life, and disinterested. As we become so affected, we tend to have problems maintaining close, personal relationships and relating with others.

2. Irritability

When affected, you will develop a shorter-than-usual fuse, fly off the handle for seemingly insignificant reasons, respond to questions in one-word sentences, usually say you are "fine" just to stop any further conversation, and keep everyone near you walking on eggshells for fear of how you will react. You may seem to be on edge, restless, and agitated. This occurs because the daily traumas of our professions tend to erode our resiliency, the ability to cope and to respond to things calmly and rationally. It is essential to let your life partner know how important it is for him or her to tell you how you may be changing. It is your job to listen to them and create an atmosphere where they will feel comfortable giving you much-needed feedback. This will help you to keep from damaging your relationship. Chapter 10 explains in detail how a life partner plays a vital role in the emotional survival of a first responder.

3. Difficulty Sleeping

Having difficulty consistently getting a good night's sleep — either because of sleep interruptions several times each night or because you are only capable of sleeping for a few hours — is a sign that you are not effectively processing stress.

4. Anger

When seriously affected, you begin to develop a pattern of taking out your stress and frustration on others, often those you care about most. You will tend to try to create a buffer around yourself, a safe zone where people will just leave you alone. You'll use anger to control others, to keep them at a distance, and to avoid taking a real look at yourself to examine what is actually going on inside.

5. Emotional Numbness, Apathy, Disengagement with Life

Becoming emotionally numb is inevitable, at least initially, and you'll need to consistently work to prevent it from overwhelming you. The job will naturally tend to make you want to shut down emotionally as a way to no longer feel the frustration, stress, pressures, and emotional pain of the job. However, this inevitably leads to seriously damaged relationships at home.

6. Lack of Communication

As you increasingly withdraw, you will tend to make the mistake of keeping everything inside. This becomes serious because, as your communication skills diminish, you will refuse to talk about how work is affecting you. Feelings of depression, anxiety, helplessness, anger, fear, and other negative emotions will then intensify.

7. Cynicism, Distrust, and Loss of Work Satisfaction

If any of the previously mentioned warning signs appear and are not addressed, you will likely become highly dissatisfied at work, extremely cynical, and distrustful of everyone in the world. This cynicism and negative outlook will send you into a downward spiral that eventually affects every aspect of your life.

8. Depression

Ignoring any of these warning signs eventually can lead to clinical depression. Left untreated, this may worsen and become potentially severe depression, resulting in substance abuse, broken families and lives, and a host of other debilitating problems, up to and including suicide.

9. Drinking as a Perceived Need ·
and Other Addictive/Compulsive Behaviors

Drinking, or compulsively consuming other substances, because of a perceived need or by habit is a major warning sign. Alcohol abuse among US police officers is about double that of the general population, with 23 percent of them seriously abusing alcohol. The military is even worse, with one study showing that 39 percent of veterans screened positive for probable alcohol abuse. Studies of firefighters demonstrate that 29 percent of active-duty firefighters have possible or probable problems with alcohol abuse. Drinking because of a need or habit tends to only intensify already serious problems and emotional issues, and it delays the resolution of real problems. If you are experiencing symptoms of post-traumatic stress disorder (chapter 7) and you drink, the chances of killing yourself increase tenfold. Alcohol consumption is one of the most damaging behaviors for first responders.

At least 20 percent of first responders will experience at least one serious addiction at some point in their career — to drinking, prescription pills or illegal drugs, gambling, sex, pornography, or many other maladaptive behaviors. If your brain becomes injured by the daily traumas of your job (PTSD), you become prone to develop an addiction. Any compulsive behavior is a major red flag of unreleased and damaging traumas.

All these warning signs present a sharp contrast to the outlook of the idealistic, positive, and enthusiastic officer who graduated from the police academy with high hopes; the firefighter who joined his engine company bursting with pride and a desire to serve; or the soldier who dreams of protecting her country. Any of these symptoms can and will become debilitating enough to change a first responder into someone their family no longer recognizes, unless they do the work to bulletproof their spirit to survive emotionally by adhering to the concepts described in this book.

The Second Component of Wellness: Self-Awareness

Part 1 of the first principle is a recognition of the warning signs. The second part is to become more self-aware, so that you will know when your spirit is suffering from the toxic effects of the job. I have experienced firsthand the tremendous change that can be achieved through the practice of emotional-survival principles. My personal story, though, is not unique. All the wellness initiatives described in this book have been shown to significantly enhance overall wellness of the mind, body, and spirit.

The solution starts with recognition of the problem and an awareness of the nine warning signs. But in order to become aware of how the job is really affecting you, you must first become aware of your inner strengths and weaknesses; what you have traditionally neglected that has hindered your wellness; where you draw support, healing, and inspiration from; and where you may need to apply more effort in order to fortify your spirit and enhance resiliency.

However, as a first responder, you are likely thinking you're fine on your own. You're probably thinking that becoming self-aware is something only weak people need to do. Yet that is the core of the problem. Your spirit is the foundation of your wellness and coping ability. If neglected, the harm to your spirit will affect every aspect of your life. Likely every one of the approximately 140 officers who killed themselves last year thought it would never happen to them. Probably every one thought there was absolutely nothing in the world that could ever cause them to take their own life; and now they're dead. Trauma can not only injure your brain (in developing PTSD), but it can kill you.

Emotional suffering or otherwise being adversely affected by the job is not a weakness but an injury ingrained in the nature of the work — one that is both fixable and preventable.

The first and most important question to ask yourself as you work toward having greater self-awareness and protecting your spirit, is this: "Do I think my job has negatively affected me and my life in any way — my health, relationships, outlook on life, and quality of life?" The two follow-up questions are, "In what ways have I been adversely affected?" and "What can I now do about it?" During the emotional-survival presentations that I have given to thousands of first responders throughout the United States and Canada, in which I ask these questions, I have yet to hear a single person assert that they have not been adversely affected by the job. Whether they are still on probation as a new hire or a twenty-five-year veteran, the answer has always been the same: a very solemn "Yes." Knowing this, do you simply ignore this fact and become resigned to your fate? Or, as is the inherent nature of first responders, do you become determined to take action, solve the problem, and not allow the nature of your work to degrade your quality of life?

It is critical that you know there are effective ways, as detailed in the forthcoming chapters, to minimize your tendency to personalize the pain, suffering, and emotional trauma you will experience throughout your career. Otherwise, you will be extremely vulnerable to suffering from one or many of the nine warning signs that your spirit is in serious trouble.

Self-Awareness Questions

Now that you have asked yourself if and how the job has adversely affected your health, relationships, outlook on life, and quality of life, the next step is to determine how you can mitigate those negative effects. Beginning here, and continued at the ends of other chapters throughout this book, are some questions listed with the intent that you take them to heart, contemplate them slowly — maybe only one at a time — and use them to ascertain the needs of your spirit. Only then will you discover a path to address those needs.

For example, consider this first question:

How do you deal with loss, pain, suffering, and a sense of helplessness? What is most effective? What else could you try?

If you have never seriously thought about this, now is the time. One of the best ways to mitigate the effects of trauma is to be prepared for it. If you have no idea how to constructively deal with suffering, loss, pain, and feeling helpless, it's important to begin working on what would be effective for you. If nothing is in place and you have not developed any coping abilities to deal with these inevitable challenges, then your spirit is unprotected. There are many different ways to deal with suffering, loss, and helplessness, many of which will be described in chapter 2. Your work is to determine what is, or what will be, useful for you. The first responder's job is replete with frustrating helplessness. We are often unable to save a life, protect a child, catch a perpetrator before he victimizes another, or turn a life around. If you are not able to face helplessness and come to terms with the limits of what you can do, then the job will consume you.

What would you do with your life if you suddenly lost your career because of a disability or any other reason? What if you suddenly and unexpectedly lost your spouse to divorce or death? How would you continue to find purpose in your life and maintain mental and emotional wellness?

This question is intended to help you focus on the one thing that is most important to you — your purpose in life that is not dependent upon anyone or anything. It is different for everyone, but you need to become centered on and connected with that intrinsic core purpose that will remain through all your challenges, losses, and trauma. When one finds meaning and purpose beyond their own self-interests, then life has real meaning. Being driven by your heart to make a positive difference throughout your service will serve to keep you well more than any other strategy.

How do you deal with a sense of loss of control? Do you try to control too many things in your life? How has trying to control people and things adversely affected your relationships and quality of life? How can you focus only on those things about yourself that you can control, such as your attitude, integrity, and reaction to things?

Since so much of the first responder's day is taken up by dealing with chaos and people out of control, we tend to try to control everyone and everything — to solve everyone's problems at home and tell everyone what to do. This question is designed to help you realize that in reality the only things people can control are their attitudes, their own reactions to things, and their integrity and compassion. Discovering how you personally deal with losing control of situations and people, without losing yourself, is an important lesson.

As another part of the self-awareness process, you should periodically have serious conversations with your life partner, at least yearly — for example, at your hiring anniversary date. Ask your life partner if you have been changing, if the job has been affecting you, and how you can help improve your relationship. Don't wait until you hear the words "What happened to you? You're not the person I married. It seems I don't even know you anymore." It would be helpful for you and your life partner to periodically review chapter 10 and all the ways a life partner can be a lifeline of support to their first-responder mate. Periodically acknowledge to your life partner that you recognize the difficulties they face in being married to you because you work as a first responder, and ask what they need from you to help them survive your career. Then tell them what you need from them so that both of you are actively helping each other survive the career.

On some level every first responder makes sacrifices for the good of others and cares for those who need them. Ideally, the knowledge that one is needed, depended upon by thousands, capable of handling any life-threatening situation, and able to provide compassionate service no matter what the threat, ennobles the spirit. But in order to wholeheartedly give and work from the heart and spirit, the spirit needs to be well.

The compassionate, noble spirit of service that lives in each first responder must be consistently recognized, nurtured, and developed to maintain that person's vitality and passion for service throughout his or her career. Consistently practicing the essential survival principles for emotional wellness will not only give you hope but will also help ensure the survival of your mind, body, and spirit so you will always be there for all those who need you.

Chapter Two

SPIRITUAL WELLNESS

Effective Methods to Shield, Nurture, and Sustain Your Spirit

It is by going down into the abyss that we recover the treasures of life. Where you stumble, there lies your treasure.

— JOSEPH CAMPBELL

Officer Lawrence quietly crept around a parked car to get a better look at the rear of a closed business while waiting for a backup officer to arrive. It was 2 AM on a very cold, foggy morning. The business's silent alarm had been activated, and Officer Lawrence thought he heard sounds of breakage coming from inside the building. He reached for his handgun, tightening his grip on the cool, damp surface.

It was now eerily quiet in the deserted mini-mall. Lawrence could almost hear the dampness collecting on his face and dripping from his nose. He saw the rear door slowly open and a head look out, then withdraw. Lawrence's heart raced as he closed his left eye to focus through his gun's sight.

A man dressed in all dark clothing came out of the building.

Officer Lawrence yelled at the man, "POLICE. STOP!" The burglar turned and fired several shots at Officer Lawrence, two just narrowly missing his head. After first ducking, Lawrence raised up and fired three shots. The intruder instantly fell to the ground, two bullet holes in his chest and one in his forehead. Lawrence saw the man slowly gasp for his last few breaths, then become still. Blood was everywhere, bubbling to the surface and pooling around the corpse. Steam rose from the blood in the cold night air, an image that would be forever imprinted on Lawrence's brain.

For the next several weeks, Lawrence saw blood everywhere. When he came home at night, he would often see blood running down the face of his five-year-old boy. Blood would suddenly appear on the dinner table while the family was gathered together eating, swirl down the drain while he was taking a shower, and even pool around his wife's head as he watched her sleep. He would see blood all over his hands and would even feel the stickiness of it even after washing his hands ten times. Lawrence had never been prepared for the fallout from such a critical incident. He was afraid he was losing his mind.

As part of his agency's wellness program, Lawrence learned of a treatment for PTSD called EMDR [eye movement desensitization and reprocessing therapy, which is explained in chapter 7]. After only two sessions, Officer Lawrence never experienced another recurrence of phantom blood. EMDR healed the traumatic injury to his brain, and he was able to process the incident and put it behind him.

Contrary to popular myth, emergency first responders are not invincible. We feel fear and are helpless at times, we suffer heartache, and we bleed just like everybody else. The concept of spiritual wellness is fairly new in our professions, but learning how to nurture, protect, and sustain your spirit is critical for survival. Following are twenty-six emotional-survival and wellness principles. All of them can help improve your coping ability, mitigate stress, prepare you to more effectively process trauma, and enhance your overall wellness.

Serve with compassion and make a difference. Search for ways to express and demonstrate service with compassion. The virtue of selfless service is fundamental in making you feel alive and useful. The most meaningful things in life cannot be seen or touched, but are felt with the heart. A compassionate way of life and serving helps us become less self-centered and more useful to others. The more we selflessly give of ourselves in kindness, caring, and service toward making a difference and fulfilling the needs of others, the more meaning, purpose, and joy we will experience in our lives and in our work.

Being useful and helpful to others while trying to make a difference with every call for service nourishes us. We should always be looking for ways to compassionately give a part of ourselves in order to fill a need, provide assistance or encouragement, and help in any way possible. An emergency first responder with a vibrant spirit is driven by the heart to solve problems, help those in need, and make the world, home, community, and work better places to be. It is important to your spirit to focus on what your spouse, children, community, work colleagues, and others need from you rather than what you want from others.

You are not your job. You have to work the job; don't be the job. If your entire identity is wrapped up in the job, then you will tend to take very personally every little thing that affects your job. This can cause great bitterness, frustration, and loss of job satisfaction. Realize that being a first responder is *not* who you are but is merely what you happen to do temporarily for a living. The essence of people is never what they do for a living. Rather, it is what kind of people they are, their character, and how they have affected others' lives. The majority of people's time should be invested in developing who they are and nurturing their spirits while sustaining deep, personal relationships with the most important individuals in their lives. Most of a person's life should be invested in what gives value to that life: those things and relationships that will be there long after work.

Many police officers, firefighters, and military personnel, in particular, have dreamed of pursuing their careers since childhood and derive tremendous satisfaction from work — at least initially. But perceiving the job as "your life" sets you up for significant disappointment, frustration, and despair. More so than most employees, first responders are in constant danger of losing their jobs because of injury. When you view your job as your life, life ends (figuratively) along with the job. Sadly and far too often, it ends literally as well.

Plan ahead. Make plans for activities with your spouse, children, and friends before you come to the end of your shift and before your days off, and work to maintain being active with them as your highest priority. Write these plans down, or you will likely not do them. Make a conscious effort to show your loved ones that they are the most important things in your day — every day. The top two regrets of retired first responders are: wishing they had spent more time with their children and spouse, and wishing they had stayed in better physical shape (by being more active).

Remain involved with your interests. Stay involved in what you found fun and interesting *before* becoming a first responder: sports, exercise, time with children, your life partner, friends outside of the profession, hobbies, recreation, coaching, reading, healthy entertainment, travel, volunteer activities, pets, time in nature — anything that breathes life into your spirit. Most first responders spend significantly more time watching television and using a computer than they did before becoming first responders.

Such activities tend to keep a person isolated and away from more productive, life-sustaining activities that nurture the soul.

Practice your faith. If you are a person of faith, do not neglect it. It has been estimated that the average first responder tends to reduce his or her church attendance or faith practices increasingly after the first few years on the job. Any faith or spiritual practice can be extremely powerful in maintaining a positive, meaningful perspective in life. This has been the single most effective practice in my own life and has enabled my spirit to emotionally survive nearly thirty years of acute stress and trauma in law enforcement. It can help keep a first responder focused on the true purpose and nobility of the work. A meaningful faith practice can significantly help keep you from becoming bitter, resentful, self-destructive, negative, or feeling hopeless and helpless. It provides a powerful counterbalance to what you experience at work, and it offers positive coping mechanisms.

Be active with others. Become involved in causes or activities that benefit others. This will help keep you active and involved with persons of similar interests while providing additional meaning to your life. It will help prevent you from becoming isolated and detached; isolation and detachment are among the first signs of becoming adversely affected by the job.

Continue practicing self-awareness. Becoming self-aware is an ongoing process. Periodically evaluate yourself introspectively. How are you changing and growing during your years on the job? Encourage your spouse and family to approach you with any concerns about your behavior since you became a first responder. Even if they don't approach you, ask them how you have changed, *and listen to the answers.*

Seek meaning and purpose. Try to determine what gives meaning and purpose to your life. What provides hope, comfort, and happiness? What are your ethics and spiritual values? How do you maintain perspective and keep in touch with the most important people in your life? In what ways do you work to improve the quality of your relationships? In what ways do you harm those relationships? In what ways do you show the most meaningful people in your life how much you value them? In what ways do you nurture your spirit? Are you drinking because you feel or believe you need to? Who and what are you responsible for, and how consistently do you fulfill that obligation?

Are you satisfied with who you are? Is your conscience at peace? What can you do proactively to improve yourself, to breathe life into your spirit, and to make yourself feel better about your character and quality of life?

Value your sleep. Get more consistent, good sleep. As I noted earlier, a study by Harvard Medical School found that 40 percent of peace officers have sleeping disorders. In addition, this study showed that, out of five thousand officers, 86 percent slept only four to six hours each night. The absolute minimum of sleep that you get each night should be seven hours, if not eight. Lack of good sleep will worsen your mood, decrease your alertness, interfere with your decision-making ability, impair your task performance, cause serious emotional and physical problems, and reduce your ability to concentrate and generally think. Eighteen hours of sustained wakefulness, according to the study, is equivalent to a .08 percent blood alcohol level.

Exercise as a way of life. Exercise consistently and refrain from self-destructive behaviors. In my experience, police officers (and other first responders) tend to reduce their level of exercise as they progress through their careers. Maintaining a consistent exercise activity level — at least thirty minutes a day, three to four times a week — is essential because it will significantly reduce your stress level, reduce your chances of getting injured, and enhance your coping abilities. Consistent exercise will reduce by 58 percent your chances of getting a heart attack or acquiring type 2 diabetes. It will also reduce tension while you're off duty and enable you to get more consistent sleep, as well as increase your metabolism rate and help prevent weight gain. Regular exercise is absolutely vital to your health, mood, and well-being.

La Mesa police lieutenant Angela DeSarro recalls an experience she had in which exercise changed her life:

After five years spent working patrol, I was selected as a crimes-of-violence detective and was soon working my first murder case. It was a brutal stabbing of a forty-six-year-old drug dealer, who had his throat slit ear to ear. During his autopsy, I noticed out of the corner of my eye, on the next autopsy table, an infant girl being taken out of her small body bag. The infant had passed away from sudden infant death syndrome and appeared to be merely sleeping peacefully, even though I knew different. I remember she had beautiful, soft eyelashes. I kept telling myself not to look at the baby as they cut her chest open to remove her heart and other organs. I couldn't look away. I watched as the forensic examiner used a special electric saw to open her skull and remove her tiny brain. I couldn't help it; I just kept looking and feeling numb.

By the end of the year I would lose track of the number of cases of senseless violence that I had worked. I had gained twenty-five pounds, was eating poorly, drinking too much, and taking antihistamines in addition to the alcohol in order to sleep. The image of those beautiful, soft eyelashes in my mind just didn't go away. I was depressed, exhausted, and completely consumed with work. In less than six years of being an officer, I was already burned out. I didn't recognize myself in photos. I was feeling weighed down not only by the physical weight gain but also by the incredible heaviness in my chest. I had grown up playing sports and had been fit all my life...until now. I remembered trying to get out of bed and feeling the weight in my stomach, and having to roll my body toward the edge of the bed in order to create enough momentum to get up. My relationship of five years soon ended. I felt dead inside, like I was just going through the motions. The job I loved so much was slowly drawing the life from my body and spirit.

I'm not sure what happened or what the catalyst for change was; I just remember waking up one morning feeling determined to save myself. I think it was the realization that the person I had become was not the person my father had raised. I was a fighter. I needed to find myself again.

I began training for a marathon: 26.2 miles, one year away. In the process of training, I began running half marathons. I lost the twenty-five pounds I had gained. I felt my physical strength return, the muscles and definition in my body return — it was a complete transformation of my mind, body, and spirit. I was passionate about something again that belonged solely to me.

Running that first marathon was the hardest thing I have ever done. A person's mind can go to very dark places at miles 20 through 26.2 of the marathon. It was the greatest physical and mental challenge of my life, and an even greater spiritual journey. Running changed me. The marathon is a great parallel to life. Being a marathon finisher, I knew there was nothing in life I couldn't accomplish, nothing I could not overcome. Running saved my life.

To date, I have run more than twenty half marathons and four full marathons. Running has provided a balance in my life. It is my outlet and my passion away from work — something we all need in this profession.

Over the years, I have offered to help coworkers train for marathons or half marathons. I promised those who committed

to a training program that I would train with them for encour-
agement. I have now trained seven employees for half mara-
thons, including a sergeant, two dispatchers, three officers,
and our chaplain. All of these people had their own reasons
for wanting to train for a run. But their reasons for running
did not matter as much as the opportunity for self-exploration,
growth, and healing. As runners gain stamina and strength,
they also build confidence, mental toughness, and an experi-
ence that acts as an incredible counterbalance to the trauma
and stress of the job.

Let go of the need to control. Focus on controlling only what you
have the ability to control. This will significantly reduce stress.
The only things in life you can control are your integrity, your
attitude, your compassion, how hard you work, your reaction to
things, and your professionalism. If you try to control anything
or anyone else, the effort will eventually control you or, worse,
cripple you.

Eat a nutritious diet. Maintain a healthy, nutritious diet. Be
careful about alcohol consumption. As mentioned earlier, first
responders who drink are at significant risk to abuse alcohol far
more than the general public. Do not abuse energy drinks or
other caffeinated beverages, since they dramatically affect the
quality of a person's sleep. Consumption of caffeine should stop
at least seven hours prior to wanting to sleep; it takes that long for
its effects to wear off. Also, processed sugar, such as in sodas, is
killing us with escalating rates of diabetes, weight gain, and heart
disease.

Build your character. The quality of a person's character is related to his or her integrity, dependability, dedication, trustworthiness, compassion, hard work, and selflessness. The quality of

anyone's character can always be improved upon. Strive each day to strengthen yours.

Consciously practice gratitude. By often remembering the truly countless things you have to be thankful for, you will naturally be kept from dwelling on all those things that could bring down your spirit. The practice of thanksgiving will help you to remain positive and deal more effectively with problems. A grateful consciousness will also help keep you connected with the people who mean the most to you, and it will aid in healing relationships.

Be humble. Practice humility, and understand that there is infinitely more to learn about any of the first-responder professions than you will ever know. Excellence depends upon constant improvement and growth. Always strive to learn more about the job, how to be more effective, and how to be more useful to your coworkers, your agency, and the community.

Just as it's good to always be looking for opportunities to learn, we should also be passionate about passing on what we know to others. Knowledge and experience is of little value when you are the only person who holds it. True influence and effectiveness is defined by what we pass on to others, and by what we do to make the agency and the level of professional service the agency provides better than when we were hired.

The practice of being humble gives a person great strength and the power to lead and influence others, and it brings peace to a person's spirit. People are naturally drawn to those who are humble, who are sincerely interested in others, always looking to improve themselves and learn, and never concerned with who gets credit or recognition.

Remain a student. Learning involves a search for truth, honesty, and a desire to positively influence others for good purposes. Learning also involves striving to keep your thoughts positive, constructive, and creative. Everything you experience, either bad or good, was first a thought. By learning ways to keep your thoughts positive, creative, and good, you can unleash your inner power to positively change and affect your circumstances.

Communicate what you're going through. It is absolutely crucial to have somebody who can share your experiences, concerns, issues, or simply what happened at work that day. All humans are social creatures who thrive on engaging with others and sharing information. First responders in particular need an outlet for expressing outwardly whatever is within them — and that includes processing critical incidents, stress, or trauma. Holding in these experiences only increases your anxiety, depression, fears, and distance from loved ones. Whether you communicate with a peer, a chaplain, a colleague or friend, a life partner, a therapist, a support group, or anyone else who gives you support, you'll find that continuous, truthful communication is essential to maintain the wellness of your spirit.

Set goals. Develop professional and personal goals that are reasonable and attainable. Lay out short-term, intermediate, and long-term goals that you can work toward every day. This will help keep work and life from stagnating. Always have a goal that you are working toward.

La Mesa police sergeant Greg Runge shares his life-plan principle:

> *It is within our nature to want to improve, to want something better for ourselves in our professional and personal lives, and to feel good about the direction of our lives. I have used a principle I call a life plan, which I reevaluate and adjust every year at New Year's. My life plan for the year is not a simple half-hearted New Year's resolution that is soon to be broken and forgotten about. It is a commitment for the entire year to work*

on specific physical, mental, financial, and spiritual goals. My objective is not so much to achieve what I had hoped to achieve by the end of the year, but to remain committed to trying every day to do something positive to fulfill my life plan.

I think it's safe to say that we all have in the back of our minds a laundry list of goals, tasks, and intentions that, if they are accomplished, will lift a serious amount of emotional and psychological weight off of our shoulders. This list seems to grow longer the older we get, and, year after year, I never seem to get around to crossing anything off. This is true for even the seemingly menial things that I've put off forever while waiting for a couple weeks off so I can tackle them — seems like that time off never happens.

Sometimes the tasks may relate to physical health, such as improving your general health, losing a specific amount of weight, running a half marathon at a certain pace, or even getting a medical procedure or some dental work done that you've been putting off. Or the goal can be a financial one — paying off a credit card, saving a certain amount of money, increasing your retirement fund contributions, or opening an educational savings account for your children. People who are close to retirement may be putting off meeting with an advisor to get a feel for how life will be financially after they stop working.

Some of the biggest tasks can be the hardest to define. These life goals are the very personal intentions that weigh on us year after year and are the most difficult to carry out. Is there a difficult conversation that you've been meaning to have with a friend or family member? An event in your past that has taken an emotional toll on you that you know you should talk about with someone, maybe even a professional? A broken relationship with a family member, friend, or coworker that you want to repair? A new hobby or interest you've been mustering the courage to try?

Then there are the mental and spiritual goals, such as studying something new, books you've been wanting to read, or improvements you want to make in your character and the strength and wellness of your spirit.

There are all manner of things that could be on your list, and everyone's list will differ. The key to making your own list is to pinpoint the life plan that, if accomplished, will make you feel better about your life. I believe the best chance to make meaningful progress in your life plan is to choose two or three areas of your life that you want to focus on during the year, and then pick one or two tasks in each area that you will commit to working on each day. Make sure your life plan for the year is reasonable and attainable. Then write it down (a yearly, month-to-month planner is perfect for this). Give yourself sensible goals and deadlines that incrementally push you toward being successful. This is your life plan for the year, and in it you will keep track of where you are, your successes, your setbacks, and, hopefully, your ultimate accomplishment — the day you cross the item off your list.

Regarding a life plan that involves character improvement and the wellness of your spirit, it is helpful to list seven to ten character traits or virtues you wish to improve upon throughout the year. Then, work on one for an entire day, then rotate to the next trait or virtue to focus on for the next day, and continue to rotate through your list one item at a time. When you've finished going through the list, start again at the beginning, and continue on this way throughout the days of the year.

The character virtues that you work on may include being more patient, letting go of anger, being more positive in your thoughts and speech, being more helpful to your spouse and *others, being more honest, being less negative in your thoughts and feelings, not wasting so much time, being more grateful, being more humble — or any other trait you desire to improve. In fact, one of the greatest minds in all of American history, Benjamin Franklin, at the age of twenty, wrote a list of thirteen character traits he wanted to work on, and he did so for the rest of his life. His life plan included moderation, justice, sincerity, peace, humility, chastity, cleanliness (in habits, thoughts, and body), industry (waste no time), silence, temperance, order, being resolute, and frugality.*

The objective of this work is to keep yourself on a trajectory of improvement. You may not meet a life-plan goal to your satisfaction at the end of the year, but through consistent effort you will have most assuredly grown closer to reaching that goal.

Discipline your will. Train yourself to make better, more positive choices that are life affirming and productive of wellness, and to refine your habits, replacing negative or harmful habits with more positive ones. Choose to express yourself in the best way you can. The practice of disciplining the will also involves consistently fulfilling resolutions and objectives, being honest in all things, and living up to all legal, moral, and ethical obligations.

Develop your sense of sincere purpose (right motivation). One of the most meaningful questions you can ask yourself is *Why?* The reason why you do something — what truly lies behind your motivation to say or do anything — reveals your true character, heart, and spirit. If your motives are not good, noble, selfless, and altruistic, then you are being controlled by your ego and selfishness. Through the discipline of right motivation, you can significantly improve your effectiveness with others, the health of your spirit, and your own quality of life.

Discipline yourself to let go. This is the practice of learning to be aware of how much you identify yourself with negative thoughts and emotions, while learning to let them go. Every time you become aware of feeling a negative emotion, you must try to replace it with a more positive one. Every negative emotion, including anger, sadness, jealousy, envy, hurt feelings, revenge, and being unforgiving, acts as a heavy weight on your spirit and significantly depletes your energy.

Become more aware of how often you reinforce negative emotions through your speech and thoughts. These habits can be changed into more positive, constructive patterns of behavior. But rather than ignoring, reinforcing, or suppressing negative thoughts and emotions, learn to acknowledge them and let them go. The book *Letting Go: The Pathway of Surrender* by Dr. David Hawkins is a valuable resource in learning how to let go of all that hinders our well-being.

Speak positively. Discover the power and influence you wield when you focus on speaking only that which is true, helpful, encouraging, and positive. People's speech is the outward expression of the quality of their thoughts, heart, and spirit.

Serve your colleagues. The training of most first responders tends to be focused on protecting and serving the community, and ironically, rarely do they see their colleagues as part of the community. Wellness in spirit is also a sense of connectedness and devotion to coworkers, who sacrifice to protect each other. Our coworkers are our brothers and sisters. They are family who deserve the utmost honor and respect. The well-being of the spirits of those who risk their lives for us, at our sides, must become one of our primary concerns. Only then can first responders coalesce together to protect each other, as well as the community, and to emotionally and spiritually survive together.

Make spiritual wellness a priority. Become proactive about developing your own spiritual-survival and wellness practices. Take an active part in developing positive habits that will sustain and enliven your spirit, as well as your physical and mental health. If you are doing nothing proactively to sustain your spirit, then you are passively allowing your spirit to decline and, eventually, suffer.

Think positively. Positive, optimistic thinking doesn't mean that you ignore reality and refuse to face difficult problems. Rather, it is a proactive approach to improving your mindset and life by practicing a more positive and constructive attitude. Instead of feeling negative, victimized, or helpless, you will, with a positive mindset, gain a higher perspective of the issue and think of constructive ways to manage or mitigate problems rather than feeling defeated. The consistent practice of positive thinking has an innate power to reduce stress, improve effective stress management, improve coping skills after trauma, reduce the intensity and duration of depression, and even improve your overall health.

If your thoughts tend to be mostly negative, your outlook on life is more likely pessimistic and defeatist. If you develop the habit of thinking and viewing life in a more positive and constructive way, then you're someone who is far more capable of sustaining a higher quality of life. Stress has been shown to be reduced by limiting negative thoughts and letting go of negative emotions.

A positive mind anticipates happiness, joy, health, success, improved opportunities, and favorable results. With a positive attitude you can experience greater hope and more pleasant feelings, and you can visualize the results you want to achieve. Your thoughts continually shape your attitudes, feelings, and quality of life, and so they affect how you deal with stress.

Practice meditation. I have been practicing meditation for nearly forty years, and I can absolutely say that the best gift you could ever give yourself is to develop the practice of daily meditation. Meditation only involves taking five to ten minutes (preferably in the morning before getting out of bed) to be still, quiet, and at peace. You can quietly focus on anything that involves a positive emotion such as gratitude or love, or maybe think of a problem and ask yourself how you might more effectively deal with it.

Science has shown that meditating for just a few minutes each day has several benefits: it reduces stress and helps to keep you calmer throughout the day; it aids concentration, keeping you focused and centered throughout the day; and it enables you to be more at peace.

Yale University has developed a course that has become one of the most popular classes in the long history of Yale: "Psychology and the Good Life." It is a semester-long course on how to have a peaceful, meaningful, happy life. This is the essence of the class's guidelines on how to realize this objective:

- Practice gratitude always; in everything be thankful.
- Practice positives: think positive, speak positive, have sustained positive beliefs.
- Remain active and engaged with life; especially be active in nature.
- Practice mindfulness, living in the present moment consistently.
- Have a purpose beyond your self-interests, such as striving to compassionately serve and to make a difference.

Following these simple guidelines in your life and service will enable you to significantly enhance your resiliency, work through most traumas, and remain motivated, healthy, and at peace.

Self-Awareness Questions for Spiritual Wellness

In what ways do you release or manage stress? Are these outlets healthy? How can you improve?

Overwhelming stress is an inevitable aspect of your work. Without effective de-stressing and coping practices, stress can eventually consume your spirit to the point where all you do each day is try to survive. That is definitely not a healthy way to live, and it will cripple your ability to provide quality service at work.

The purpose of this question is for you to consider not only how stressed you have become but also all the contributing stressors you experience each day. Then, rather than merely reacting to being stressed, you can evaluate what proactive steps you can take to process and reduce your stress levels. The many stressors are not going to go away, but you can learn how to work through the feeling of stress, process it, and release more of it in order to keep your spirit from being weighed down.

Do you feel the "need" to drink or consume any other substance? Do you need alcohol to sleep, to enjoy yourself, or to relax? Can you do without alcohol or some other substance for three days without feeling any effects? (If not, a potentially serious problem is developing.)

This question is designed to help you realize whether you have become dependent on alcohol or another substance and, if you have, to find a positive way to heal your spirit. Often first responders don't realize how dependent they have become on alcohol or other substances just to function — to sleep, to relax, to enjoy life. If you perceive as a need the consumption of anything other than what is medically required, then you have become dependent on it. Such dependence is typically a symptom that your spirit is suffering and needs your attention.

What can you do to enhance your mental, physical, emotional, and spiritual well-being?

Finding just one thing you can do to enhance each of these components that make you human will help to increase your survivability and odds of making it to retirement and being well.

Chapter Three

EMOTIONAL WELLNESS

Overcoming Hypervigilance

Every trial endured and weathered in the right spirit
makes a soul nobler and stronger than it was before.

— JAMES BUCKHAM

La Mesa, 2013. Within fifteen minutes of ending his shift, Terry, an emergency medical technician, was inside a liquor store, just as he was every day at the same time. Terry was a nine-year veteran of the fire department who worked as a paramedic. He had also served two tours in Afghanistan in the US Army Reserves. When Terry was first sent to Afghanistan, he had hoped that being away would help him finally forget the images of a three-year-old child laying face up at the bottom of a bathtub immersed in scalding water that was still steaming and far too hot to even touch. Terry burned his own hands taking the dead child out, who had been held in scalding water by his father as a punishment until he died and his suffering ended. The image of the innocent child with his bright-red body and loose skin seemed to constantly be in Terry's mind. But far from helping, serving in Afghanistan — with its sights of children blown up by suicide bombers just for attending school — haunted him as well. Terry was constantly on alert in order to remain alive or to help keep others alive.

Terry had no practical emotional-survival training. The acute stress a paramedic experiences — while always having to be perfect to prevent others from losing their lives — kept him on edge constantly while at work. This hypervigilance, coupled with unforgettable images, made him feel as if he could never rest, never be at peace. He thought the only way to keep the images away and relax was to drink himself to sleep or unconsciousness. Initially, after about a year on the job, Terry had begun to drink more than before as a way of trying to relax and to get some sleep. Then alcohol slowly became a physical and psychological need, leading him down a hopelessly dark path.

Terry's wife of eight years couldn't take it any longer and had left him six months earlier. She had told him that she didn't marry a drunk, that she was tired of having her life constantly affected by Terry's terrifying images, his nightmares that seemed to never end, and his drunkenness. She could no longer watch him come home only to vegetate and grow ever more distant, unapproachable, and disengaged. She told Terry more than once that he had turned into someone she no longer recognized — or liked.

Now all alone at home with his bottle in his hands to comfort him, Terry couldn't wait to begin to forget as he tried to unwind; it was now the only thing in his life that he looked forward to.

The high-intensity psychological and emotional level of alertness and aggressiveness that first responders need in order to stay safe on the job is called *hypervigilance*. First responders are trained to be constantly aware, always on guard — to consistently seek out and evaluate potential threats. The hypervigilant state is necessary on the job, but cannot be easily turned on and off like a switch. Because hypervigilance is ingrained in the work, it is one of the most difficult aspects of the job for first responders to overcome in their personal lives.

As Kevin Gilmartin describes in his popular book, *Emotional Survival for Law Enforcement*, this intensely elevated level of alertness causes an automatic neurophysiological reaction in the mind and body after a first responder leaves work. In order for their mind and body to return from this hypervigilant state to the normal functioning range, the body produces an equally intense opposite reaction to bring the person down.

In other words, while at work, first responders are extraordinarily alert, perceptive, active, constantly making decisions, and engaged in their task, and this state can feel pleasant or even euphoric to them. When they go home, where hypervigilance is no longer needed, their minds and bodies naturally feel exhausted. Emergency first responders tend to not want to make decisions or become interested in others in their downtime, and this can lead to their becoming isolated, apathetic, and detached. Unfortunately, the downside of the hypervigilance cycle also decreases the metabolic rate, often causing first responders to gain weight.

Gilmartin has found that normally it takes about twenty-four hours for the mind and body to recover and return to their normal functioning range. By then, however, the first responders are already back at work in full hypervigilance mode once again. By the weekend, they are so exhausted by this roller coaster that it can take most of their days off to recover. If not properly managed, the cycle can have a devastating effect on a first responder's quality of life, emotional wellness, and personal relationships over the course of their careers.

It is imperative that first responders develop certain practices and conscious mechanisms to make their off-duty thoughts and reactions more socially conforming. It is less a matter of turning off the first-responder mindset than turning on and tuning in to a civilian mindset, where they enjoy the company of the people closest to them and see others as benign rather than as threats.

Law-enforcement agencies in particular train their officers to be cynical about everything, to distrust human nature and people's motives. That worldview is essential if officers are to keep safe and to stay alive on the job. However, what's essential for physical survival at work can become devastating to first responders' home lives and emotional well-being. If a spouse or children become as strangers, it is because the first responder has estranged them by allowing the negative aspects of the profession to emotionally separate them from those they need most. When first responders treat the good people in their lives in the same way they treat the ones they encounter on the street while on duty, they alienate themselves from those who could provide a lifeline of support and critical care for them.

Both human nature and the motives of the people who are close to first responders are essentially good. First responders must learn how *not* to see everyone as a criminal, how *not* to be distrustful of family, friends, and children, to realize that about 98 percent of the people in the world are basically law-abiding citizens not out to harm others. Unfortunately, many first responders tend to make poor choices in order to maintain the good feelings of the hypervigilant state. They do this by not going home, by working an unusual amount of overtime, drinking away from home with colleagues, and engaging in promiscuity and other high-risk behaviors. They unfortunately tend to become less invested in their family relationships and less interested in doing the things they used to enjoy. And a consistent state of apathy, isolation, fatigue, and detachment can lead to depression or substance abuse.

Emergency first responders who are single parents or caregivers face greater challenges to survive emotionally. Whether they're caring for elderly parents or struggling with health issues or behavior problems with children, these first responders are rarely given the opportunity to come home and just unwind or do something else solely for themselves and their own well-being. This makes it more critical that they proactively maintain daily wellness practices and express what they need to allow the hypervigilance cycle to balance itself. It is important for them to create a mental and emotional break from their work mindset to focus on affirming the good that they can do for themselves, either through mindfulness meditation or other practices, so they can be their best for those who depend upon them at home.

It is imperative for *all* emergency first responders to recognize and come to terms with the hypervigilance cycle. They cannot escape it or pretend it doesn't affect them; but they can proactively manage it and prevent it from causing them irreparable harm.

Emotional-Wellness Strategies

The ten emotional-wellness strategies that follow will assist you in managing the hypervigilance cycle and in maintaining your energy, your activities, and your general interest in life.

1. Control Your Personal Time

Create your own techniques for managing personal time. When you don't make plans well in advance, then you allow work and emotional stress to control your time. Aggressively and proactively plan ahead for off-duty family and personal time, long *before* your days off and before the end of your shift. If plans are not written down and scheduled, they are far less likely to happen. So write them down. Schedule well in advance those things that nurture your spirit and show loved ones that they are the most important part of your day.

Keep your personal life separate from the job. Your personal life does not just take care of itself. If left unattended, it will deteriorate. Take responsibility for maintaining, nurturing, and enjoying your personal life. Your personal life is, in fact, your "real" life and should only be complemented by your job as a first responder. Rather than passively allowing work stress and the demands of the job to control your true life, learn to live for your time away from work, when you can breathe life into your spirit and renew your emotional wellness.

Show your love by your specific behavior and by spending quality time with loved ones. Show them how much you value them — don't just tell them. Family members need to know how important they are to you, and you can demonstrate this in different ways each day — by how often and the way you talk with them, what you do with them, and how often you include them in your life.

2. Live Life as a Survivor, Not a Victim

Do not allow the job to drain the life out of you or make you bitter, angry, frustrated, and apathetic. The job should be life affirming. First responders work in a profession that few are entrusted to perform; they protect and give life to others so that everyone can live in security and peace. First responders affect people's lives every day, and they have the potential to create a positive interaction with every contact and to make a positive difference.

Focus only on what you can control. You can control only your own integrity, how hard you work, your own attitude, your reactions to things, your compassion, and your professionalism. Most stress in life is caused by resisting, suppressing, or fighting the things that really can't be controlled. Learn to accept what you have no control over, and practice letting go. Accept what is, while striving to positively and constructively improve things — or at least your reaction to things that can't be changed.

Develop the habit of asking a constructive question when you come up against an issue that makes you feel like a victim. Rather than excessively complaining and becoming bitter and cynical, ask yourself questions like "What can I do to positively change the situation and improve things?" or "How can I keep this from adversely affecting me?" Then, take control and work to improve the situation.

Live in the present moment. People who thrive tend to live in the present moment, neither dwelling on the past nor living in the future. Don't waste your time and energy on guilt or regret or on anxiety about the future. Learn to forgive yourself, make up for past wrongs as best you can, and move forward. Try not to resist current circumstances, but find ways you can positively influence them without trying to control events or other people.

3. Relate to the True Purpose of Your Profession

First responders are a force for good in society, the ones who fight evil and those who prey upon the innocent. They keep society in order and allow our way of life to continue. There is nobility and honor inherent in all the emergency-first-responder professions. Our nation and community need you to be emotionally and spiritually well in order to provide the essential services of protection.

In the course of his or her career, every officer saves hundreds, if not thousands, of people from being victimized. Never forget the lives you have saved, helped, protected, and positively influenced. Remind yourself before every shift that you have the opportunity to make a positive difference in every life that you touch. Focus on what the community, agency, fellow officers, and others need from you, and on how you can fulfill those needs — *not* on what you need or want from them.

4. Proactively Control Your Finances

If you need to consistently work overtime to pay the mortgage and utilities, then your financial obligations have total control over you. Your goal should be to resist further irrational spending and whittle away at debt. Practice living within your means, and your stress will significantly diminish.

5. Consistently Get Restful, Uninterrupted Sleep

The Harvard study of five thousand police officers, mentioned earlier, assessed officers' on-duty performances for two years. The 40 percent of the officers surveyed who reported undiagnosed sleep disorders experienced sleep apnea, insomnia, and sleep deprivation. The prevalence of sleep disorders showed a corresponding and significant adverse effect on officers' overall health, including increased susceptibility to diabetes, hypertension, heart disease, depression, burnout, and emotional disorders.

The study showed that officers with sleep disorders were 25 percent more likely to express uncontrolled anger to a suspect or other citizen, and were 35 percent more likely to have a citizen complaint filed against them. Sleep-deprived officers were 51 percent more likely to fall asleep while driving on duty than officers who were not sleep deprived. Of all officers in the study, 25 percent reported falling asleep at the wheel once or twice a month. "Drowsy driving" may help explain why car accidents have overtaken criminal assaults as the second leading cause of death among police officers (suicide being the leading cause).

One in three officers have sleep apnea, a disorder that causes a person to wake up repeatedly because breathing has temporarily stopped. That's at least eight times higher than the rate among the general population, and it is a serious condition. The surprisingly high incidence of sleep apnea has grave implications for officers and their agencies. The disorder taxes the heart because the sudden jolt when waking up is accompanied by a surge of adrenaline, which is believed to lead to cardiovascular disease. Officers with sleep apnea have 90 percent greater likelihood of developing cardiovascular disease, even when adjustments are made for their age, sex, body mass index, and smoking and other risk factors. Officers with sleep apnea also had much higher risk than other officers of developing diabetes (61 percent), depression (150 percent), and emotional burnout (270 percent), and experienced a greater risk of falling asleep while driving home from work (126 percent).

The most effective way to prevent sleep disorders is for officers to exercise consistently, eat properly, avoid working excessive hours, and especially, avoid abusing alcohol or energy drinks and other caffeinated beverages. Being well rested will also serve to keep you interested in staying active.

6. Plan for Retirement from the Beginning of Your Career

It's crucial for you to be thinking about and planning for your retirement from the moment you are hired and throughout your career. A major emotional trap for first responders is that they tend to strongly identify with their job; and when the job is gone, often their identity and reason for living are gone. Your job can disappear at any moment because of injury or a number of other unforeseen circumstances. Having a financial plan, as well as activities and interests beyond your first-responder career, helps to keep you grounded and focused on the continuation of life outside your career.

Take advantage of deferred compensation plans or other savings and retirement plans. Plan for the possibility of not being able to work, as well as for remaining active in life after retirement. Suicides and other emotional suffering among first responders significantly intensify shortly after retirement or after becoming disabled, often because there was no preparation or planning. Without long-term preparation, people can easily find themselves feeling lost, disconnected from life, and emotionally desolate as they struggle to find a purpose in life beyond work.

Review your retirement plans each year at the anniversary of your hiring. Work toward realistic retirement objectives while you're still employed. Always have a goal in sight.

7. Eliminate or Reduce Alcohol Consumption and/or Other Substance Abuse

Few things that first responders do cause more potentially serious problems for their careers, families, and emotional survival than abusing alcohol or any other substance. The choices made as a result of drinking, the adverse effects on your quality of life, work, and health — all these make it more difficult to effectively maintain the wellness of your spirit. Substance intoxication only exacerbates hypervigilance, hindering the body's own natural means of readjusting. Over the long term, symptoms of PTSD and feelings of depression, despair, or hopelessness will ultimately only intensify with drinking. Drinking in moderation may be all right, but most first responders have no idea what drinking in moderation really is. The bottom line: if you feel you need to do it and you can't limit it or stop when you try, then it's harming you.

8. Resist the Maladaptive Coping Escape of Promiscuity

Many first responders use promiscuous sexual behavior as an escape or as a means to maintain the euphoric feeling of the hypervigilance cycle. As in the case of excessive drinking and substance abuse, promiscuous behavior is a sign of deeper emotional issues that aren't being dealt with in a constructive manner. These behaviors demonstrate poor coping abilities that need to be recognized and addressed.

Incidents of promiscuous behavior tend to increase with PTSD and other emotional issues, as well as with problems in dealing with the hypervigilance cycle. This can be devastating to a person's family and career, and especially to a first responder's own emotional survival and well-being. Ultimately, there is a significant emotional cost: regret, guilt, loss of integrity, and loss of self-respect.

9. Practice Relaxation Techniques, Including Meditation and Visualization

Along with the emotional trauma and acute stress of a first responder's job, there always seem to be incessant demands and distractions that weigh heavily on your spirit. If you don't take time to consistently practice relaxation and stress-reduction techniques, you'll find it difficult to overcome the hypervigilance cycle. Zoning out in front of the television or computer screen may mask underlying pressures, but it actually does very little to alleviate stress. To promote the nervous system's relaxation response, you'll need to engage in a mentally active process that leaves the body relaxed, calm, centered, and focused.

Consistently practicing relaxation techniques reduces stress symptoms by slowing your heart rate, lowering your blood pressure, slowing your breathing rate, increasing blood flow to major muscles, reducing muscle tension and chronic pain, improving your concentration, reducing anger and frustration, and boosting your confidence in handling problems.

Healthy, effective methods of relaxation involve a short, specific time period in which you focus on relaxing and reducing stress. Effective methods include the following:

Meditation. When you catch yourself feeling pressured and thinking about your job, your relationships, or your endless to-do list, practice letting the thoughts escape while stilling yourself and sitting quietly, free of all distractions, with your eyes closed, while taking slow, deep breaths for about five to ten minutes. One form of meditation entails sitting in silence and focusing your thoughts on peaceful memories and positive thoughts and feelings. Meditating for five to ten minutes when you awaken is a great way to start the day more relaxed, focused, and centered on what you would like to achieve that day. The idea is to take your mind off your stress and focus it instead on an image that evokes a sense of calmness. The more realistic your visualization is in terms of colors, sights, sounds, and even physical sensations, the more relaxation you'll experience. Some people of faith find it useful to use meditation each day for a few minutes to connect with their source of unlimited hope, inspiration, and purpose. Spiritual meditation and prayer connect a person to a higher calling, an inner purpose in life that sustains, heals, offers peace, and boosts a person's resilience.

Music. When things get rough, take a detour by aligning your heartbeat with the slow tempo of a relaxing song. Listening to music, especially slow, quiet classical music (by composers such as Debussy, Grieg, Handel, Mendelssohn, Dvorak, Sibelius, Franck, Bach, or Gounod), can have a tremendously relaxing effect on your mind and body. This type of music can have a beneficial effect on your physiological functions, slowing the pulse and heart rate, lowering blood pressure, and decreasing the levels of stress hormones.

Visualization. While sitting quietly for five to ten minutes with your eyes closed, hold the mental image of a positive outcome to a problem, or the image of a peaceful place you have visited or would like to visit, or in your mind's eye watch the stress leaving your body. Creatively visualize anything that helps you to relax and calm your breathing.

Progressive muscle relaxation. While sitting comfortably and silently with your eyes closed, focus on slowly tensing and then relaxing each muscle group, starting with your toes and slowly working your way to your neck and face. This helps you become aware of physical sensations while focusing on the difference between muscle tension and relaxation. Tense your muscles for at least five seconds, and then relax for thirty seconds, and repeat. Do this while breathing deeply and slowly.

Tactical breathing / deep breathing. This technique can be practiced anywhere at any time. It has been shown to immediately reduce stress symptoms and can help alleviate certain symptoms of trauma. Practice inhaling slowly and very deeply through your nose with a breath as large as you can intake. Hold your breath for a count of four, then slowly release all the air through your mouth. Repeat this four times.

10. Serve with Purpose and Compassion

Compassion in service refers to actively trying to make a difference while looking beyond the minimum effort necessary to handle a particular incident. Often, listening to someone longer, taking extra time to provide assistance or advice, and offering words of comfort or hope can significantly affect someone, potentially for years. Helping someone feel better, providing guidance, and caring for someone's well-being beyond what's expected demonstrates our capacity to serve with compassion, which gives life to our work and spirit and helps to reduce the stress of hypervigilance.

This approach was perfectly illustrated by a chance encounter by one of my own officers. Officer Mike Hughes responded to a radio call requesting medical aid for an elderly couple at their home. The wife, Susan, was suffering from congestive heart failure and was having difficulty breathing. Her seventy-three-year-old husband, Ted, was distraught at the distress of his wife. Usually, with these types of calls the officers merely stand by and offer assistance to the medics while they work on the patient and transport them to the hospital. Officers go to hundreds of these types of calls, stay for a few minutes, and move on to handle other things. But this call would be different, and the result renewed and healed the spirits of many who served.

While standing inside the house, Mike was overcome by the nauseating stench of the place; it nearly took his breath away. Obviously, this couple was extremely poor. The house had decayed flooring and practically no furniture at all, was filled with dust, dirt, and filth, and was severely in need of repairs. There was mold all over several of the walls as well as on the wood floors. Rather than being disgusted by the place and getting out as soon as possible, Mike was moved by the couple's plight.

As he took an interest in them and began to ask the distraught husband questions, Mike learned that the couple had not had anything to eat, other than a sandwich, in the past four days. There was no food anywhere in the house. He learned, too, that they had not been able to afford trash pickup for the past three years. The rear patio and backyard were filled with trash and hopelessly overgrown with weeds. When things got too bad, Ted would fill a trash bag and walk around the neighborhood late at night to look for a partly empty trash can that one of his neighbors had set out that he could fit some of the trash into. Susan and Ted's washing machine and dryer had not worked in more than two years. The gas and electricity was about to be turned off, and the house heater was inoperable. Officer Mike Hughes understood the meaning of compassionate service and how important it is not only to the person helped but also to his own spirit and wellness. After Susan was taken to the hospital, Mike had Ted get into his patrol car. He drove him to the nearest grocery store and used his own money to get all the food and necessities the couple needed. He then got his sergeant involved, who used his own money to establish future food deliveries to the couple from a local church's food bank. After dropping off the groceries at the house, Mike then drove Ted to the Salvation Army Ray and Joan Kroc Corps Community Center and was able to obtain several more food items for the couple. Mike even had his wife make homemade lasagna and casseroles for the couple, which Mike delivered.

Two days later, after hearing about what Mike had done, I went over to Susan and Ted's home to check on them. Susan had come home from the hospital. I, too, was taken aback by the condition of their home and how they were living, so I drove Ted to a store and got him more supplies. Then I contacted Maxine, one of the police department's civilian employees, and had her meet me at the house. Maxine immediately became involved and arranged to have someone work on the couple's washing machine and dryer. They were fixed within days. Maxine got a social worker involved with the couple to see what other services might be available. Maxine arranged for donations and had trash service reestablished for an entire year, and she also worked to have the electric bill reduced and paid up to date. I treated and got rid of all the mold and painted a lot of the interior of the house. Mostly, I spent time with the couple, visiting them several times a week for months, helping them out with groceries or money for rent when it was needed.

Maxine, in coordination with the police department's chaplain (and volunteers from her church), then arranged for a cleanup-and-repair date, with nearly a dozen police department employees helping out. In one day, several teams worked to clean and repair the entire house, and to clear the patio, the backyard, and the rest of the property of trash and weeds. Since then, police employees have periodically gone over to check on the couple to see how they are doing and if they need anything. When they do, employees donate money, items, or time to help out.

Recently when I spoke to Ted and he was thanking us for what everyone had done, he had tears in his eyes. As he fought back the tears, he said, "I didn't think anyone would ever give a damn about us. Thank you."

A few weeks later Ted passed away from lung and bone cancer. With the added expenses, Susan could pay little, if any, of her rent. We gathered some money and paid the rent for her.

I then took a look at the rental contract and saw that the landlord had handwritten the words "as is" at the top. I searched through the Business and Professions Code and discovered that even if a house is rented "as is," it still legally has to have a working heater, smoke detectors, working plumbing, and no rotted floors or mold anywhere. The law authorizes a $500 fine for every violation.

I met with the landlord and showed him the multiple thousands of dollars of fines he was facing. I told him, "Look, I'm a captain and I can make all of this go away. All you have to do is agree to reduce her rent by five hundred dollars a month forever." He looked at the fines and he agreed to lower her rent. She never had to worry about rent again.

What so many of my fellow employees experienced in serving

and helping the couple will no doubt stay with them throughout their careers. Having this kind of a positive impact on someone, in the midst of all the negative and depressing things we deal with every day, dramatically nurtured and ennobled our spirits. It gave meaning to our work and satisfied our spirits in a way that sustains us and helps relieve some of the stress of hypervigilance.

We don't often get the chance to save a life, but we can affect many every day, one call after another. While serving with their hearts, first responders can find ways to help, inspire, and provide hope and comfort to others through their words, actions, and examples. The most effective officers are those driven by their hearts; this is the essence of service and the sign of a vibrant spirit. First responders should have incidents of compassion like this to remember during their retirement, rather than struggling to forget all the other aspects of their careers.

The adverse effects of hypervigilance can be very much mitigated by focusing on what I term character-based service. This refers to a first responder serving with a purpose by following these five guidelines:

1. Remember that your profession is a vocation of the heart and that to prevent your heart from suffocating and shutting down, you need to always be serving with your heart to make a difference wherever you can.
2. Dedicate yourself to providing selfless service, solving problems, effecting positive change, and fulfilling the needs of others in order to promote the greater good beyond your self-interests.
3. Always serve with integrity, meaning doing the most-right thing, being compassionate and life affirming, always being honest in your actions and speech, and rightfully doing all that is expected of you.
4. Always remember the purpose and nobility of your work.

5. Always strive toward self-improvement. Also, make a personal commitment to pass on everything you've learned to make others and the service of your agency more professional and effective.

My Story: How I Cured My Own Hypervigilance

As I look back to my stepdaughter's eighth birthday party in 1996 and that critical realization of how emotionally dead, exhausted, and disengaged I had become, I recognize that it was truly a crossroads in my career and my life. I came perilously close to losing all connection with the person I had been when I was hired by the police department. Hypervigilance, stress, and other pressures of the job had overwhelmed me, and I was losing my ability to enjoy life.

My journey of self-discovery and learning how to emotionally survive would not be easy. It has been a career-long effort to learn from others, become more aware of what my spirit needs in order to thrive, and practice various methods and techniques centered on emotional survival.

Things would get worse before they improved. I would answer the door (on those few times I ever answered the door) with my service gun in the small of my back — just in case. I avoided crowds and looked forward to simply going home and resting. After receiving death threats while working the James Desmond murder case, I began watching for someone outside as the garage door slowly opened every morning. I made sure my wife and stepdaughters knew to leave me alone when I was home. I withdrew from several activities I had once loved. I often got less than four hours' sleep a night while I obsessed about the case I happened to be working on. And eventually, after ten years of marriage, I found myself divorced while raising one of my stepdaughters alone. A second marriage also ended in divorce.

Fortunately, I discovered that one of the most effective facilitators of mental, physical, and spiritual wellness was physical activity. Consistent physical exercise clearly counteracts the adverse effects of the hypervigilance cycle more than anything else. I began running much more consistently, bought a bicycle to begin long-distance riding, rediscovered my love of the ocean and swimming, became an avid snorkeler, and began hiking more frequently. I developed a love for the national parks and, over the years, have explored dozens of them from Alaska to Florida.

I discovered the significant healing potential found in the peace and serenity of nature. Nature has an inherent ability to humble us, to take us away from ourselves and center us in its beauty and peace. Experiencing nature enabled me to purify my spirit, to become inspired, renewed, and connected with life. Each one of these activities breathed new life into my spirit and renewed my sense of wellness. They enhanced my ability to cope with and process emotional pain while managing the hypervigilance cycle. I learned that this had to be an ongoing process to prevent my emotional fuel tank from getting drained.

One of the most important things I did was immerse myself in activities with my stepchildren (I remarried and gained two stepsons). There is nothing that will lift and heal your spirit more than spending time with your kids, loving and enjoying them, while showing them every day how important they are to your life. Your problems seem to fade away as you look into a child's smiling face. I also began volunteering as a basketball coach, which had been a lifelong dream.

I searched for new outdoor activities I could become involved with. I took sailing lessons and began sailing whenever I had the opportunity. I had lived in San Diego my entire life but had never kayaked or surfed. I have since kayaked all over the San Diego area and now, at age fifty, I am learning how to surf. I also took up skiing and make it a point to go on ski trips every winter.

I will always remember the time when I was working a patrol car at three o'clock in the morning, trying once again to keep from falling asleep or driving into the curb. For some reason, I got out of the car to look at a war memorial at the local VFW. This memorial is one block away from the police station, and I had driven past it numerous times a day for twelve years, yet I had never once gotten out to read it. I found that the memorial listed the names of every La Mesa resident who had been killed in the Vietnam War. At the bottom of the memorial was an inscription: "Have you lived your life worthy of someone else's sacrifice?" This greatly influenced me as I realized how much we owe those who have come before us. And it inspired me to keep focused on the solemn duty of my work as a first responder and on how I can affect the lives of others.

Over the years I developed another of my greatest interests: writing. I discovered the power of words — their ability to inspire, influence, and change a life. I usually have several interesting books on hand that I'm actively reading, always looking for opportunities to learn, experience, and pass on what I've learned to those I supervise and work with.

I also discovered that the more I expressed compassion, and the more opportunities I found to volunteer and support and help others, the less I felt disconnected or affected by work trauma or stress. I've sponsored several children overseas for over twenty-six years and have volunteered in nursing homes, at church, at animal shelters, and with other organizations. Being in the company of animals, being in nature, and volunteering with kids all have the uncanny ability to remove us from ourselves and the world around us. The one thing first responders need is to be removed from their world from time to time.

Living love, selflessly giving, and serving others truly do heal the spirit and are extremely powerful in overcoming depression, isolation, emotional pain, and self-destructive tendencies. Most first responders were inspired to be first responders because of a desire to help others, to make a positive difference in people's lives. As the acute stress and emotional trauma of the job increases over the years, our motivation to serve is often the first to suffer. Focusing on serving others and being devoted to the greater good will keep you balanced, positive, and emotionally well.

I helped coordinate a summer youth leadership camp where officers facilitate a weeklong camp for high school kids to teach them about leadership, ethics, and community service. (If you are interested in developing your own version of a youth leadership camp, the FBI has published an article on our program, its curriculum, and its effects. See https://leb.fbi.gov/articles/featured -articles/police-youth-leadership-camp-influencing-young-lives.) I've also coordinated my agency's efforts to adopt a middle school where over three hundred students live under the poverty line. We provided computers, books, and sports items donated by local businesses, and we started a running club with officers for the students. For more than twenty years I have coordinated the police department's efforts to adopt needy families during Christmastime to provide much-needed food and toys. Over the years we have helped more than sixty families, with over $15,000 raised among the officers and dispatchers. For twenty-three years I have coordinated a food drive for the needy at Thanksgiving. All these efforts have helped me to forget about the darkness of the profession while striving to be a light to others.

Over the years, I have practiced nearly every suggestion described in this book, some more than others. But all have been effective in helping me remain driven to serve with my heart and maintain wellness. We should never forget that behind our badge is our heart, and our heart needs to be steadfastly put into our service for us to survive and be well. It is vital for individuals to discover their own best practices when cultivating emotional survival and wellness. Whatever practices work for you, engage in them consistently throughout your career and life. The most critical of your emotional-survival and wellness practices is your focus on the wellness of all of the components that make you human: your mind, your body, and, particularly, your spirit.

I always looked forward to coming to work every day. After thirty years, I remained passionate about the work we do to protect life. I remain positive and hopeful for the future. No one is destined to become a victim of a career in public service. When we learn to protect our spirits and serve with purposed compassion, a life of service ennobles and enlivens us.

Self-Awareness Questions
to Help You Overcome Hypervigilance

What do you do for others, and what more can you do? Do you treat others the way they want to be treated, focusing on their needs and not on yours?

While recovering from hypervigilance, you will find that the natural tendency is to become self-absorbed. You'll tend to think more about yourself as you zone out in an endless effort to feel relaxed and rested. Develop the habit of paying more attention to the needs of those around you, and not only will this help you remain active and feel useful, but it will also help you keep out of the disengaged trance of the hypervigilance recovery period.

How do you deal with anger, frustration, ingratitude, and personal affronts? How can you deal with these emotions more positively and constructively? In what ways can you learn to let go?

When you are conditioned to react instinctively to personal affronts, anger, and frustration, the ensuing emotional response is usually negative and not helpful. Training yourself to remain centered in a place of peace within will help you not to overreact or become overly angry and frustrated with the stress of events and people. In answering these questions, you can discover a more constructive outlet for handling these feelings.

At the end of each day, are you able to look back and honestly say you did your best for your spouse, your kids, your work, and others who depend on you? If not, why not, and what can you do the following day to improve?

We improve through self-examination. Without asking yourself where and how you could have done better, you are likely not to notice. An inherent gratification and peace arise when you feel that you either have done your best or are working toward being your best.

Do you truly love your work?

When I ask this question in my trainings throughout the country, maybe about one-third or so will say they absolutely love their work. Sometimes, almost no one admits to loving their first-responder job. Yet typically every person will say they loved the work when they first started. What happens?

To survive your service career, you must find something to love about it beyond your self-interests. There is so much to love about service and about protecting and giving life to others. I looked forward to my police job every single day of my thirty-year career. I miss it every day now that I'm retired. Strive to never lose sight of the fun and all there is to love about a career in public service.

Discover your "Why?" Why do you want to do this job that is so dangerous when it threatens your life, health, peace, and wellness? Why do you do this job, with the difficult shiftwork, and with not being understood or appreciated by much of the public or often by your own agency's administration? A first-responder job is one of the most difficult, dangerous, and toxic jobs out there; but it is also, I sincerely believe, the best, most fulfilling, and most fun — as long as you can be in tune with a reason, a purpose to do this work. Find your purpose, learn to remain in love with this work, don't take things personally, and you'll likely discover how fulfilling it truly is.

Chapter Four

TRAUMA, POST-TRAUMATIC STRESS, AND THE PROCESS OF HEALING

---

he entire physical world is nothing more than our classroom, but the challenge to each of us in this classroom is...will you make choices that enhance your spirit or those that drain your power?

— CAROLINE MYSS

After thirteen years on the job, San Diego County Sheriff's Deputy Mike Spears became involved in a thirteen-minute gunfight with a child molester. Mike and his partners went to arrest the suspect, who had filmed himself having sex with his six- and eight-year-old stepdaughters after having been offered $50,000 for the film. The molester had been warned that the police were coming to his home. He got out his high-powered military rifle and his armor-piercing rounds; he closed all the blinds, turned out the lights, and lay down in his hallway with the rifle trained on the front door, just waiting for the police to enter.

Three officers went to the front door; Mike was in the middle. As the police entered, the first officer was shot twice, once in the upper arm and once through the upper chest and shoulder area, leaving an exit wound nearly the size of a grapefruit. The officer fell onto the floor far inside the apartment. While bleeding profusely he continued to return fire, but he was shooting in the dark, unable to see the suspect who continued his rapid-firing assault on the officers.

While Mike was engaging the suspect and trying to reach and rescue his fallen partner, the third officer behind Mike was suddenly hit and became incapacitated. Mike immediately thought that all three of them were about to die.

Mike was not able to get far enough inside the apartment to rescue the initial critically wounded officer. Mike decided the only way to survive was to make a tactical retreat. While dodging bullets and continuing to shoot toward the suspect, Mike grabbed the wounded officer behind him and began dragging him out to get him to safety. As Mike was backing away, the suspect crawled to the door and began closing it, trapping Mike's other, more critically wounded partner inside. As the door was closing, Mike made eye contact with his wounded friend, who said, "Don't leave me here. Come get me." Then the door closed, and the gunshots continued.

Mike kicked in the door of a neighboring apartment and pulled the one wounded officer to a place of relative safety. Then Mike immediately returned to engage the suspect. A thirteen-minute gunfight ensued, during which a rescue team was formed. Eventually everyone was rescued, and all miraculously survived. The suspect now is serving life in prison for multiple counts of attempted murder of a police officer.

Mike's partners have physically healed. Mike never received a scratch but was deeply wounded by his traumatic experiences. His invisible wounds of trauma still haunt him, though he is continuing to improve and heal.

Below is Mike's own account about his struggle with post-traumatic stress. He offers extremely useful insights into trauma and the process of healing.

Trauma is any experience that can significantly affect us in a negative way over a long period of time. As first responders, we have such experiences every day at work. Some are severe, others less so, but all such traumatic experiences have the potential to injure our brain. When the brain's processing ability has been injured by either a traumatic incident or an accumulation of such incidents, symptoms of post-traumatic stress can develop.

Trauma can not only injure your brain; it can kill you. That's why suicide continues to be the number one cause of death for first responders. It is beyond terrifying to lose all control over your life and lose the ability to function normally.

You don't have to be involved in a shooting to develop PTSD. Every day we experience traumas that over time can injure our brain. Most first responders who suffer from PTSD were never in a shooting, were never involved in anything horrific. In most cases, traumatic day-to-day experiences are the cause.

The good news is that, as an injury, PTSD can be healed. [See chapter 7 for effective treatments for post-traumatic stress.] As first responders, we are all vulnerable. No one is invincible. The more you practice the wellness and healing strategies in this book and from other resources, the better prepared you will be and the more resiliency you will have, so that hopefully you will not suffer in the ways I have.

After my shooting I became numb, depressed, anxious, distraught. I was unable to sleep, and I had uncontrollable emotions and intrusive thoughts I couldn't make go away. I'd never had anxiety or been depressed before. I became someone I didn't recognize, unable to function and be normal. I lost all control over my emotions, thoughts, and ability to relate to others.

I secluded myself from my family, including my wife and children, as well as my friends. I didn't want to talk with anyone. A couple of things kept me alive; one of them was CrossFit. I was an avid CrossFitter before the shooting, and it helped save my life after the shooting. For several months after the shooting, I would come home after a CrossFit workout and go straight into my room and shut the door. I would remain isolated inside the room with no lights on, sitting in the dark, watching Netflix movies all day. I didn't want to talk to my wife; I didn't want to talk with my two little daughters. I would just sit alone in the dark.

I tried to be "normal" in that situation, but normal wasn't my normal anymore. My marriage suffered because I wanted my wife to act a certain way toward me and she didn't, and that crushed me. What I really wanted and needed was for her to comfort me, but I never told her that. I just remained distant. She, in return, knew I was upset and didn't know what to do; so, feeling helpless, she just left me alone.

I can tell you that your spouse, life partner, or kids can become victimized by your profession just as much as you can. You need to tell them what you want because you can't expect them to intuitively know what you need. This is critically important: Tell your life partner what you need from them. Do not suffer alone in silence. Not only can it kill your marriage, but it can kill you.

I've been diagnosed with post-traumatic stress disorder. I don't know why it's called a disorder. It's an injury. From the trauma I experienced, I have an injury in my brain that inhibits its ability to process life and to be normal. It affects every *part of my life, and I deal with it every day since my shooting, though things are steadily improving.*

I have experienced the severe effect that trauma can have on the brain. As I understand it, very simply put, the brain has three main layers: the primal, which primarily deals with fight, flight, or freeze; the amygdala, which deals with emotions and the ability to relate to people and communicate; and the neocortex, which deals with reasoning, logic, and thinking.

When the processing ability of your brain has been injured by trauma, the primal layer becomes overactive, while the amygdala and neocortex become much less active. This results in your feeling the anxiety, fear, agitation, panic, and terror of constantly being in a fight-or-flight situation, while your ability to experience normal emotions and to think clearly are very much inhibited.

Imagine seeing an antelope desperately running for its life, looking back with enlarged eyes of terror as a lion is pouncing on it from behind. Now, imagine that same antelope feeling all those terror emotions and running for its life — yet there is no lion. That's how your injured brain functions and what it's like having PTSD.

However, I'm here to tell you that it is impossible to run away from PTSD. You can never outrun it; you have to stop, face it, and deal with it to regain control over your life. Things will not get better with time if you do nothing to heal your brain.

The first step is to admit that something has happened to you and it's affecting your life; then seek help either by seeking EMDR therapy or another PTSD trauma therapy that can restore your brain's normal functioning. Such therapy treatments work to release the negative effects of trauma from your brain and central nervous system, restoring your health, wellness, and sense of peace.

This is how my traumatic injury has affected me: depression, anxiety, suicidal thoughts. I'm not a man who would kill myself, but I had suicidal thoughts every day for years after the shooting. Beforehand I never once thought of suicide; I was never depressed. Now it is just a part of my life until I get well. I've thought of all the different ways I could kill myself. I can say I definitely wouldn't do something to have another officer take my life because I don't want anyone to live with the things I live with.

You have to learn to deal with it. You have to develop coping mechanisms, hopefully before your brain ever becomes injured. If you can, surf, work out, play golf, hike, camp, be with your family — do something to take your mind off the job. You need an outlet away from work to survive this career. You have a long time in your career. You have to work the job; don't be the job. You should enjoy your job, but you should enjoy your life much more.

To develop PTSD, you don't necessarily have to be involved in a shooting or another major horrific incident. Every day you're doing something that's traumatic. You see things that other people don't see. You deal with things others don't ever have to deal with; and then you have to go home and be normal. You can't let this job eat you alive. You have to have faith. You have to have the spiritual mind. You have to have a healthy physical body; and you have to have mental health. Your mental fitness is most important. You can be physically fit. I feel great in my body, but my mind plays tricks on me a lot. If your brain becomes injured due to trauma, it will have a mind of its own; and it's terrifying.

I have learned that if you have symptoms of PTSD and you drink, your chances of killing yourself are ten times greater. Drinking while suffering from PTSD (as well as isolating yourself) is about the worst thing you can do.

I know of a California Highway Patrol officer who was involved in a fight for his life. He nearly died, and the fight ended with him having to kill the suspect. He and his wife give speeches about how that trauma has affected him and their marriage. Prior to this incident they had been married for twelve years, and the officer never once cheated on his wife. After the traumatic incident, the officer repeatedly cheated on her, with multiple women. Now, with a deeper understanding of how trauma affects the brain and can lead to addictions, they are working together to put their marriage and life back together.

Officers affected by trauma are in danger of becoming addicted to all kinds of destructive behaviors, including drinking, gambling, taking prescription or illegal drugs, and sex or pornography. Basically, if it is possible to become addicted to something, first responders have found a way. The reason for this is that while you're engaged in such repetitive, maladaptive behaviors, the overactive primal layer of your brain tends to calm down, making you feel better. You feel some relief from the imbalances of your brain. As soon as you're not engaged in that activity, the primal layer of the brain returns to being overactive and uncontrollable.

However, such behaviors only tend to offer very momentary relief, while their effects are extremely caustic, dangerous, and long lasting. Until the underlying causes of your symptoms are treated and healed, the symptoms are likely to continue and even worsen. You cannot outlast PTSD; the symptoms do not eventually just go away without you first doing something to heal from the underlying traumas that have caused them.

I've learned to cope with the suicidal thoughts and the feelings of depression and anxiety. I let them happen without resisting or fighting against them. Then I affirm something positive as a way to let them go, such as "That's not helpful" or "That's not me. All will be well." Because if I let the negative feelings eat at me and eat at me and eat at me, they can destroy me; and I'm not going to let that happen.

If you feel something different, something you don't like that's going on inside, say something so that you can get help. If a colleague is suddenly acting differently, you need to say something to get them help. Because we owe it to ourselves — and to those we serve with and depend upon for our own life and safety. Everyone in our profession has been affected by trauma. Every single first responder has been changed in many ways by the nature of their job. If something is bothering you, you need to talk to someone about it. You can't keep ignoring the issues and hiding them. It is impossible to run away from the effects of trauma; please face and deal with them.

The biggest thing for me is that after my shooting everything I had ever experienced in my career came to the surface. Everything just exploded, and I suddenly found myself reliving past upsetting experiences. Over and over again, my shooting replayed in my head, and I kept reliving scenes of dead bodies and all the other terrible incidents I'd seen.

For the first few years of my career, I worked for the San Diego Police in a high–gang crime area. Shootings, stabbings, and gang fights happened daily, nightly. I was dealing with dead bodies in the street, with people who had committed suicide, with gang violence and robberies. It all takes a toll on you, and yet you're still supposed to live life normally. I beg you, if you need help or if you know somebody who needs help, get it out in the open and talk about it.

About three weeks after my shooting ordeal, I was fixing a broken bathroom door handle at home. The door was closed, and my wife and two daughters were in the hallway behind me. All of a sudden, I heard a loud boom and I "saw" the door splinter open in the center with a bullet coming directly at me in very slow motion. Terrified, I jumped back to avoid the bullet. I looked back at my family as the bullet was still coming toward my chest.

I see things that aren't real all the time since my shooting. I never know when it will happen or how it was triggered. It just happens, and I feel all the terror and panic as if it were actually happening to me. It is beyond terrifying to lose control of your life, of your thoughts and emotions. You feel hopelessly lost and helpless.

When these things happen, I get very angry. I've been angry all the time since my shooting. I get angry when I think about suicide. I get angry when I get depressed. I get angry when I feel anxious and can't function — because I know that isn't me. I have all these emotions that I never experienced before. I'll be driving down the street sometimes and I'll just start crying. I don't know why or what triggered it, but I just cry.

There have been a couple of incidents where I'm driving and my daughter is sitting next to me. We're just driving straight, going through a green light, and then all of a sudden, I see a car come across and crash into my daughter's side of the car. It's not happening; I'm driving with a green light. But I "see" this occur in my mind's eye, and then I see my daughter fall into my lap dead, with parts of her brain on me. And the anger gets to me again. I get so angry when I have these thoughts and feelings that were never a part of me before. I just have to look over at my daughter and tell her I love her. She looks up at me and says, "I love you too, Papa." And then I try to just move on.

To heal yourself, you need to take time for yourself, and even when you don't feel like it you need to force yourself to remain involved, active, and engaged with others and with life. Don't do what I did and isolate yourself. Tell people what you need from them. In each moment try to do the next right thing. Find ways to keep moving forward with your healing and with your life. You're not losing your mind. What you feel is a normal result of what you have experienced. It's not about what's wrong with you; it's all about what happened to you, and you can heal and get well as I am doing.

There is a process to healing and taking care of yourself. The biggest thing about healing is that if you don't tell anyone that you have a problem, then it is going to eat away at you. You have to admit that something is going on inside that you do not like. It could be a small matter, but small matters ignored will often turn into large issues we can't ignore.

Please don't be caught unaware. The traumas you experience every day at work can suffocate your heart and can not only injure your brain but erode your ability to function, be well, be at peace, and relate to others. You don't have to be in a shooting to suffer from the job.

As a perfect example, I once arrived at the scene of a major accident in which an off-duty California Highway Patrol officer crashed the rented vehicle he was driving that also contained his wife, her brother, and their fourteen-year-old daughter. Initially I didn't even know it was a crash; I thought it was a brush fire when I just happened to come upon it. I was there for four hours watching these people burn to death in the car. At the time I thought they were alive, but they weren't; they had died on impact.

Immediately after those four hours at the accident scene, my first radio call was to attend to a twenty-seven-year-old man who overdosed on heroin and died in his mother's arms. So I went from one extreme situation to another. How do you deal with that? How do you process that, along with all the other traumas of your everyday work life, unless you are pro-active about your physical, mental, emotional, and spiritual health and wellness?

First of all, you have to tell the people closest to you what you need because people can't read each other's minds. My wife thought I needed to be left alone because I was upset, when what I really needed from her was support and comfort. But I never told her that; I just stayed distant and isolated. As I look back, she needed support as well, but I never gave it to her.

Our family members are potentially victimized by our pro- fession just as much as we can be victimized by the traumas we experience. You need to support your family members, ask them what they need from you, and tell them what you need from them. Work together to survive this career and find ways to continue to enjoy life together.

Our jobs make us cynical. We see things we don't want to see all the time. For most of us, initially we did the job because we loved it, and then we end up hating the job because we come to hate people, since we see almost everyone as an idiot or a criminal. Ninety percent of the population we deal with are not very good people. Dealing with them becomes like listening to a broken record, over and over again, day in and day out. Many of the calls are the same, but they're different in their negative effects upon us. You can become jaded and calloused — you see every call for service as just another call. You don't want to make that difference any longer.

You have to keep making that difference and remain driven by your heart to help where you can and to be useful. If you are not actively trying to make a positive difference with each call, the job is going to eat you alive. With every single service call, strive to make a difference. Whether it is a kid who crashed on a bike or a homicide scene, whatever it is, make a difference.

I often think about how much further I would be in my healing process if I had only known beforehand how essential it was not to isolate myself. How much better off would I be if I'd known how vital it is to remain engaged and active with life, with friends and family? How much further along would I be if I'd known how critical it was to tell my wife what I so desperately needed from her?

Please don't wait until you're suffering from trauma and post-traumatic stress before you start practicing wellness strategies. They need to become a natural part of your life and service; enhancing and strengthening resiliency, remaining motivated, processing trauma, and enhancing the quality of your life and service need to be part of your daily routine. Learn from what I have experienced and take your wellness seriously. It's not inevitable that you will suffer from this job; but chances are you will if you don't do anything proactively to enhance your ability to heal, to serve with compassion, and to be at peace.

To view Mike Spears sharing his story on YouTube for free, go to YouTube and enter "Mike Spears PTSD."

Self-Awareness Questions for Healing from Trauma and Post-traumatic Stress

Do you have any symptoms of PTSD?

Go to www.ptsd.va.gov to learn all about trauma, stress, PTSD, symptoms, treatment options, and how to get help for both you and your loved ones.

Are you aware of the resources available to you through your agency, peer support, and community? Does your life partner know of these resources as well?

Find out what resources are available to you and your family, and how to access them prior to ever needing them. Knowing that there is help available, and where to go to find it, is crucial for a quicker and more complete recovery and healing. Also, www.emdria.org is a great resource where you can find trauma therapists trained in EMDR (an extremely effective treatment for PTSD) in your area. Also, a Google search for "EMDR trauma therapists" in your local area will bring up additional certified EMDR trauma experts.

Chapter Five

SURVIVAL LESSONS

Live as if you were to die tomorrow.
Learn as if you were to live forever.
— MOHANDAS GANDHI

It was another slow night in La Mesa, which, back in the nineties, was a sleepy suburb. Diane, an emergency services dispatcher, was the lone 911 call taker and dispatcher on duty. Since nothing much was going on, Diane was making plans for her family's upcoming vacation. She was thinking how nice it would be to get away and relax; she hadn't had a vacation in nearly ten months.

As Diane was imagining the white sands of southern Florida, the 911 line rang. It was the first call she'd had in an hour. Diane reached for the phone, and as she raised it to her ear, she could hear the blood-curdling shriek of a woman screaming for help. "9-1-1. Do you need police or medics? What's happening?" she asked in an urgent but professional tone. There was no answer; it sounded as though the caller had dropped the phone. But the screams continued more faintly, possibly from another room.

"Stop! Please don't do this. Please don't kill me. I'm begging you...Please don't hurt me! Somebody please help me!" The unknown woman continued to scream as she desperately begged for her life. Diane immediately dispatched the entire squad to the address that appeared on the 911 screen while continuing to yell into the phone in a desperate attempt to get someone on the line.

The police racing toward the house across town had no idea that an enraged ex had broken into his estranged girlfriend's house and caught her with another man. The suspect had already shot the other man several times and killed him, and was now threatening to kill his former girlfriend. Diane heard a disembodied male voice calmly tell the woman that he had warned her, and that now she was going to pay. The terrorized woman repeatedly pleaded for her life as Diane continued helplessly to try to get someone's attention on the phone. Suddenly, she heard one shot, followed by immediate silence.

Diane yelled into the phone. "Is anyone there? Is anyone there?" Then she heard the cold, emotionless voice of the suspect when he picked up the phone and said, "It's too late," and then, almost casually, "What the hell," and shot himself in the head. The absolute quiet was soon shattered by the sound of sirens — police arriving on the scene.

This horror show had played out as Diane sat helplessly by, unable to affect the outcome. Worse yet, it was soon discovered that the two murder victims were young police officers from a neighboring agency, and the suspect was a police officer from another county. Diane had never been prepared for an experience like this. She continued to work as a dispatcher for nearly a *decade before switching to another job within the department. Today, after more than twenty years on the job, the voices she heard that night still haunt her.*

We can learn a number of invaluable lessons from our first-responder colleagues who struggle with the same frustrations, debilitating stress, trauma, critical incidents, and sense of helplessness that we all are constantly exposed to. An integral aspect of wellness training is learning from the experiences — both good and bad — of others who have come before us. Learning how other first responders effectively process the trauma of the job is crucial.

An Emotional-Wellness Study and Its Practical Applications

In recent years a number of troubling incidents have plagued the police department in San Diego, the nation's eighth-largest city. In the year 2011 alone, three officers were murdered, one committed suicide, two died in accidents while off duty, and a dozen faced legal charges for everything from fixing tickets to sexual assault. An extensive study of the department attempted to pinpoint the causes of acute stress and discord among the officers, which are prevalent within all the first-responder professions.

Prompted by the police department's newly established wellness unit, Julia Holladay undertook a major research project for the University of San Diego in 2012. The two thousand officers of the San Diego Police Department police a city with a population of more than 1.3 million people. The study centered on problems that tend to cause significant stress and emotional trauma throughout the police department. The researchers conducted personal interviews with the officers, the most direct way to ascertain the quality of their subjects' spiritual and emotional wellness and extrapolate the most helpful, practical methods for survival. Following is a collection of some of the most-often-cited concerns and lessons from the officers, concerning issues typical of any emergency-first-responder agency. All the quoted statements in the remainder of this chapter are from the actual study participants. Their insights and lessons are just as pertinent to any first-responder job, not just the police. Trauma affects us all, no matter how we experience it, and the strategies to work through and release its effects are universally useful.

Struggling against Hypervigilance

"I do try to leave work at work, but I didn't think trauma was affecting me in my home life. I don't want to lose control. I go to houses to help others cope, and I'm losing control of my own home."

This is the insidious nature of the first responder's job. The damage is like a slow, malignant tumor growing in your consciousness and spirit. Before you realize it, you become overbearing and obsessive about controlling people. You begin to treat your spouse and family like criminals, suspecting everyone and everything.

A first responder avoids "losing control" of his or her home by making every effort to remain engaged in the activities and interests of those at home. You don't deserve to be treated any differently because of your job. Your family needs you and deserves to have you physically, mentally, emotionally, and spiritually present and engaged with them consistently, without your trying to control them.

"You always look for people with an ulterior motive. You eventually don't trust anyone anymore, and you always look at the 'what if.' You become extremely cynical. I am aware of so many things that people do — things that it would be better not to know. It's hard to turn that knowledge off."

It's important for officers to remember that being an officer is a job; it is not who they are. The love they experience with their families and friends away from work, as well as their active pursuits outside of work, are what breathes life into their spirits. Most people are basically good and have good intentions. Not everyone is a criminal.

"Here at work, you need a command presence and hypervigilance. On patrol or taking a radio call, you have to make split-second decisions, so you are ramped up and expedient. When you go home you are still in it, mentally and physically, and you have to make that shift. If you don't catch yourself, you begin making quick decisions and people at home don't want you to fix it. They may just want you to listen."

This is an extremely important point. As a first responder, you are expected to solve everyone's problems quickly, to be assertive, and take care of business. However, this doesn't work in our personal relationships. Your spouse and children do not want you to solve all their problems. They mainly want and need you to listen to them, to offer emotional support, and to be there for them in the way they want and need, not respond in the way you would on the job.

"The stress comes home with me. But you have to learn how to shut it off. Off duty you are always on, and the stress can kill you."

You need to realize the value of balance and keeping the proper perspective. Like everything else in life, balancing conflicting interests and responsibilities is essential to maintaining the wellness of your spirit. As another officer said:

"You have to realize the damage this job has the potential of doing and cultivate the ability to adjust to it to stay healthy."

Resist Shutting Down and Disengaging from Your Family

"I used to come home and shut down. I would come home and feel like a zombie, just wanting to sit and watch TV and not do anything else.

Now I try and take a lot of time off. I like to spend it with my kids, but it's harder to make it work with my wife."

"Before, in the first year on the job, I was really shut off. I was engaged that year, and my fiancée told me how she felt like she was walking on eggshells around me. I don't want someone to feel that way around me, so it was definitely good feedback. If you don't know the problem, it's hard to fix. It wasn't hard to open up once I did. I just didn't want to expose others to my issues, but then I thought, 'Hey, if they are opening up to me, it's not fair not to open up myself.'"

"Problems start when you let things get out of hand, like drinking too much or being promiscuous. Some guys keep things bottled up and then blow up. They don't include their wife or family in things. When I talk to my wife, she is totally aware of what's going on, whereas a lot of my friends have wives who are totally clueless. Keeping it in internally and not including family makes it hard."

Any first responders who are in doubt about how they have changed and how the job has negatively affected them need only ask their life partners. Spouses will typically say they no longer understand their first-responder mates. They don't like what their mates have become. They describe their mates as shutting down immediately upon coming home. Their mates don't talk or share anything about work, are always tired, moody, and disengaged, and want to be left alone. The spouses can rarely get them to participate in making family decisions, even something as simple as where to go out to eat. These first responders use a favorite chair like a baby uses a pacifier. Spouses don't know what they can talk about with their first-responder mates, when to bring up issues or problems, or how to get their attention in general. These spouses also complain about their partners never wanting to do anything fun or to spend time with neighbors and friends outside the first-responder profession.

All these comments are typical, and they clearly demonstrate the serious relationship and emotional problems that can arise if work stress is not addressed. It is true that your spouse can never understand what you experience at work — and this is probably a good thing. You should not try to make your spouse understand. When your spouse greets you and asks about your day, he or she doesn't want to hear the details of the child molestation case you worked or what the mangled bodies in the accident looked like. What your spouse really wants and needs to know is *how you are doing* — to know that you are all right and to understand generally how the day affected you and if there is anything he or she can do to help.

If you had a particularly emotionally troubling day, it's all right to say you worked a tough case that is really troubling you. Let your spouse know what is going on inside you and what specifically they can do to support you. Your spouse needs to be your greatest source of support, comfort, and peace; don't push them away! Allow them to connect with you the way they need to, and in return, they will typically do anything in their power for you.

Also, take time off from work to spend with your family. It is such a waste when officers retire with hundreds or thousands of hours of vacation and allotted time off still on the books. Periodically use your time off to replenish your soul and to spend meaningful time with your family. Our families need to be our greatest support networks. You must consistently find ways to be engaged and involved, to be a genuine partner to the one who cares the most about you and who needs you to be well.

"I believe in the book Emotional Survival for Law Enforcement *[by Kevin Gilmartin] and see a lot of myself and other officers in that book. It should be part of the curriculum in the academy and tested on, because it could save careers and marriages. In fact, the whole family should read it."*

Books like this and *I Love a Cop: What Police Families Need to Know* by Ellen Kirschman offer great information not only for the first responder but also for the spouse and family. It is critical for the spouse to become involved in supporting the first-responder partner. A spouse learning how to best support and care for their first-responder mate can significantly assist the first responder in remaining emotionally well and healthy. (More specific information on how life partners can best support their first-responder mates is included in chapter 10.)

Constantly Guard against Stress, Depression, and Isolating Yourself

"If you're alive, you've survived [...but, I would ask, if you are just surviving, are you truly alive?]. The adrenaline has its highs and lows, and part of the balance is having an outlet and people to talk to. A physical outlet will help to some degree, but you need an emotional outlet, too.

"I feel like I want to be a hermit. I am usually someone who likes to be out doing something, biking, hiking, walking my dog. I still function, but when I feel this way I am not in the happy place of feeling normal — my normal."

"Police work has higher stress than most jobs, and the stress builds unless you remain active. If I don't go run and instead stay home like a couch potato, I don't have an outlet for my stress."

It is essential to think ahead, and to write down your plans to be active on your days off. Otherwise, the winding down from the hypervigilance cycle that's such an integral aspect of the first responder's job will control you and keep you from making the effort to be active. It is vital to keep doing the things you enjoy, before you develop the habit of not doing them.

Workplace Gossip, though Commonplace,
Is Detrimental to Officer Morale

"It is emotionally and mentally painful to be on the end of the gossip chain."

"In a nutshell, I can deal with people outside this division, the citizens, and the criminals; it was the people under this roof that I couldn't deal with — bad-mouthing me and getting in the way of my career."

The worst thing first responders do to each other is deride one another. This has devastating effects on the morale of individuals and the agency as a whole. Any first responder who participates in gossip, derision, and spreading rumors is actively participating in sabotaging the spirit and well-being of one of their own. This recklessness is a cancer within the agency, and people should be called out when they so carelessly act to harm the very people they depend on for their own protection, for their very lives.

As one police officer put it:

"We can take a life in a moment's notice; so we have to have trust, to look after each other and do it honorably."

Available Support Services:
Can They Be Accessed Confidentially?

Police culture places a high value on appearing strong and self-sufficient, and it tends to stigmatize anyone who asks for help. Unfortunately, officers tend to prefer to handle problems privately.

"I am supposed to know how to help others. I don't want to be 'that guy' with the dysfunction. I guess I haven't felt I've needed to ask, and I didn't want to be one of 'them.'"

In contrast, another officer stated:

"You have to understand you are not going to be weak if you ask for help. A peer-support team member was my mentor. He didn't sugarcoat stuff and actually cared. Being humble has a lot to do with it."

Humility is one of the greatest character virtues. It will help you maintain the wellness of your spirit so that, as a first responder, you can survive and thrive in your profession. It is essential to step back from the image of being a superman or superwoman and realize that you are human like everyone else. You're just as vulnerable and just as susceptible (if not more so) to pain, suffering, and emotional trauma. No one is capable of doing any first-responder job without it potentially changing them and making a significant impact on their emotional wellness and spirit.

If your leg were seriously hurting you, you would go to the doctor. When your spirit is suffering, you are in even greater need of healing. Emotional trauma isn't a weakness; it's an injury to the brain and spirit, to a person's ability to effectively process traumatic circumstances. And it is not a sign of weakness to seek help from a trusted coworker, a chaplain, a peer-support team member, or a counseling service. *It is a sign of courage.* In fact, allowing yourself to hurt, and allowing your loved ones to needlessly suffer because you won't seek the help you may temporarily need, is a tragic sign of weakness. Any assistance is there to help you be well, to be the best you can be for others — not only for your family but also for your colleagues and the thousands of people in the community who depend for their survival on your being mentally, physically, emotionally, and spiritually well. You will be unable to meet anyone's needs if you stubbornly (and stupidly) refuse to meet your own.

"For someone I am close to in the department, I would suggest getting help: go do it. For myself, I would get help if I needed it, but wouldn't tell anyone. There are resources available, but when is the culture actually going to change?"

"You are supposed to be the one helping and not asking for help. From what I've heard from others in the past, those who needed help were looked at negatively. Today, there seems to be less of a stigma, because I've heard officers talk about the help that is available. I went for help after a shooting because I was second-guessing what I could have done differently. Counseling was incredible, because I got to debrief full-on, talking about the entire incident from beginning to end with my wife sitting there, which made her understand everything."

"Often officers internalize and think to themselves: 'I'm tough. I have no weaknesses. I can take care of myself.' Because officers who survive the job learn how to identify what's wrong, they can then seek help and find the tools to make things better."

"We are the ones giving help and [are] not supposed to be the ones to get help."

This is a common perception, but unless you are not human, there are experiences that will trouble your soul or possibly torment you. Anyone's brain and thought processes can be injured by experiencing a traumatic event. Being well is a good thing. Part of being tough — and smart — is becoming self-aware and honestly evaluating what you need while being strong enough to seek assistance.

"We don't want to be seen as weak amongst our peers and that's the stigma. If you want and need to get help, your ego says, 'No, you don't need help.' You have to get outside that voice, rise above it, and if you really need it — get the help. We want to be seen as strong and self-sufficient, and we guard our privacy."

You can always maintain your privacy while doing the right thing and making an effort to seek the confidential help that may be needed. The important thing to remember is that tens of thousands of first responders are needlessly suffering from PTSD, acute stress, and depression because they choose not to get assistance. The mind and body react in many different ways as they try to process acute stress or a traumatic experience — ways that we just don't understand. Resisting, suppressing, and concealing that which is troubling you will not make it go away but will intensify the symptoms.

"I needed to go to the counseling service. I made an appointment and the therapist gave me a test to see how depressed I was. Out of a score between 1 and 10, I got an 8, which is high. I didn't even know I was depressed, and that's scary. It goes to lack of awareness, not as much about stigma."

"Those who don't get help get depressed and then begin not to care, so they drink, gamble, use drugs, and go down the cesspool that can lead to suicide — all because they won't get help."

The tough persona of first responders has resulted in the senseless deaths of more officers than all of the assaults, killings, and accidents many times over. Every year, suicide is the leading cause of death among officers. Is it all right to know inside that you lost your career, your spouse, your spirit, everything that you loved, but that at least you're still a tough person? Pride doesn't actually help when your career or life is spiraling out of control. Real men and women do what is needed in order to be well so they can take care of those who need and love them.

"Officers who don't have access to resources get so stressed and backed into a corner — yeah, that's scary. Maybe that's why suicide rates are so high among officers? There is a correlation between the two. When officers get into trouble like that [recent criminal and suicide incidents within the department], they were probably not seeing someone for help. Sure, others may notice signs, but the person wasn't seeking help."

"I went to the Counseling Services for work trauma and a resulting drinking problem; that was the hardest thing I ever did. I would get off of work at 4 PM and be at the bar by 4:10. How I made it home without being pulled over I will never know."

This officer undoubtedly saved his career by being aware, being smart, and getting help when nothing else was working. Drinking, substance abuse, promiscuity, depression, and gambling are symptoms of an underlying cause — typically acute stress or emotional trauma — that has not been effectively processed in a healthy manner.

Support from Peers and Senior Colleagues Is Invaluable

"The stigma is that you are not in control and there must be something wrong with you. Peer support [by] officers on critical incidents helps, because you are hearing from a fellow cop who understands that if you get a full plate, it is okay to ask for or seek other help. This stigma is hard to overcome because cops feel like they have to handle anything that comes their way. The department fosters independent thought. Having the wellness unit and other viable resources with peers to talk to or people with experience is helpful. The job can have a negative effect, and if you don't have support it can get to a boiling point and affect you professionally and personally."

"I think if an officer is approached by a supervisor, mentor, or someone who is genuinely interested in their well-being, he may be more likely to get necessary help than if left to his own devices."

This is why it is imperative for supervisors and officers to take a personal interest in the wellness of those they work with and depend upon. First responders must pay attention to each other and actively look for ways to show concern and to take better care of one another. Compassionately showing genuine concern for your fellow officers could significantly help others deal with whatever issues they may have; it could save a career — or a life.

Talking with peers who have experienced similar things, or seeking help elsewhere, is often the very thing necessary for understanding and healing to occur. That is why a peer-support team is essential, even critical, for every first-responder agency. Details of the many benefits of a peer-support team, as well as how to form and maintain such a team, are described in chapter 9.

"I had one officer tell me he was going to bill me for all the help he was giving me through my divorce. He is just a buddy, a really good guy. He used to text me and call me to check up on me and would say, 'Let's meet for lunch.' He reached out to me, and I didn't have to ask him. I am the type who won't ask for help, unless I am offered. When I know I need it, I'll take it."

This is a great example of how first responders must look out for and help each other. What a great way to assist a coworker going through a tough time. First responders need to always remember that their survival depends on their brothers and sisters working at their sides. Our colleagues' well-being is in our best interests. We all depend on each other for life and for the opportunity to reach retirement with a healthy and strong spirit.

Cultivate Strong Relationships and Interests
Outside Your Agency

"I think that some officers take their job too seriously. What I mean by that is that the job is their life. They do not have anything else outside the department. Officers need non-work-related outlets; otherwise it will eat them alive. Also, I don't think people actually grasp what they are getting into when they start this job."

"The job is what I do, not who I am, because in the beginning I would think, 'I'm a cop...I'm a cop.' I am not that way anymore. I am still proud of what I do, but it isn't everything anymore."

"I have pictures of my kids in my office for a reason: they are plastered on my wall to remind me why I am doing this and who depends upon me."

"Outside interests are huge. Officers say they have friends who are not cops, but it is scary how many really don't. They can't admit it to

themselves. I know an officer friend who retired a few years ago and he is lost because all of his friends were officers and they work."

"I have close friends who are not PD because it gives me a big reality check. Not everyone is a dirtbag, a suspect out to get you, and there is kindness in the world. It keeps me grounded not to be with police department people. I have friends who are close enough to me to tell me that, 'No, you are not rolling down my window so you can yell at that guy,' or 'Stop eyeing someone who looks suspicious.'"

"There have to be roles that are more important than being a cop [or any first responder]. There are roles like husband, father, coach, or youth leader, something more important because the job doesn't last forever."

"In terms of surviving emotionally, you have to have strong social bonds, loving and caring relationships, and a solid support group. Without support, you'll fall. I also have friends outside the department."

"I see that some officers who retire die soon after because they don't have other interests and their whole life has been about being a cop, and that's all they know. I've always had something, other interests."

The Importance of Emotional and Spiritual Survival

"Self-awareness is key, and a good officer has this."

"I sometimes observe officers and think to myself, 'He's never going to retire.' You see what mistakes they are making and can just tell that they will do something to sabotage it. There were over eighty people in my police academy, and there are only eleven of us left."

"Trainees see me as easygoing and talk to me. I try and tell some that this job isn't for everybody and there is no shame in deciding you don't want to deal with this. Bad outcomes are many: domestic violence, alcoholism, suicide. The stuff that goes into this job takes its toll."

"It's hard because we can't control everything. Successful officers know that there are some things that just can't be controlled no matter how hard we try. You have to learn to let go."

And finally:

"The bottom line is you have to care about people. It's not all about putting people in jail."

As this extensive university study on one major police department demonstrates, the need for you to focus on your spiritual-survival and wellness practices is clearly evident. We can learn invaluable lessons from those who work at our sides, themselves struggling to try to find ways to maintain wellness.

Self-Awareness Questions to Improve Your Personal Relationships

What are your most important personal relationships, and what makes them important?

Maintaining support through your personal relationships is essential. This question is designed to help you discover which relationships are the most important and what you derive from them. Once this is understood, you can work at not taking these relationships for granted and can actively pursue enhancing them for your own lifeline and wellness.

How can you improve your most important relationships? What can you do to heal hurt relationships and make up for past wrongs?

Learning to let go, forgiving, and asking for forgiveness are important elements in a healthy and mature relationship.

Where have you personally found comfort? How do you comfort and help others?

First responders desperately need comfort and to feel at peace. If you discover and remember what gives you comfort, you will be less likely to ignore it. Seek out what gives you peace — what comforts and consoles you. Then, you will be better able to comfort others, which in turn will nourish your spirit.

Chapter Six

THE SPIRITUALITY OF SERVICE

Compassionate, Life Affirming, and Productive of Wellness

I serve to be of some use for the greater good of others.
I no longer live for what I want, but in how I can serve
by keeping others in the sanctuary of my heart.

— ANONYMOUS

During an early September morning in Albuquerque, New Mexico, police officer Ryan Holets responded to a radio call about a petty theft that had just occurred in a convenience store. Most officers would have handled this routine call in a few minutes and moved on to do something else less mundane, but Ryan was always looking to make a difference.

As Ryan left the store, he noticed out of the corner of his eye a couple sitting on the grass against the building. Both were in the act of shooting heroin into their arms. As he approached them, Ryan saw that the woman was about eight months pregnant.

Thirty-five-year-old Chrystal Champ looked up at Officer Holets with sunken, ghostly eyes that couldn't conceal years of addiction and hopelessness. Ryan yelled at her to stop, telling her she was going to kill her baby. Chrystal just lowered her head and began crying. Through her tears she told Officer Holets that she knew she was a horrible person but that she had been homeless and addicted to heroin and methamphetamine for over fifteen years. She said the drugs controlled every moment of her life and that she had to continue doing heroin to keep from getting sick. "This is my life. I do it to put off dying."

Chrystal told Officer Holets that she desperately hoped that maybe someone would adopt her baby and give it a chance at life. In that moment, Ryan no longer saw a worthless, homeless drug addict but a desperate mother, a suffering woman who had lost all hope. Ryan was always trying to make a difference in his service as an officer, and this was a chance to help and do much more.

Officer Holets opened his wallet and showed Chrystal a photo of his wife and four children, including a ten-month-old baby, and in that moment, he offered to adopt her baby. Ryan drove home in his police car and told his wife what he just experienced. He asked if they could adopt the baby, and his wife, knowing her husband's heart, never hesitated.

Hope Holets was born three weeks later. Ryan was at the hospital for the delivery and kept thinking back to the surreal turn of events that had brought him to this moment with a pregnant homeless heroin addict. Two days later, Ryan and his wife gave Chrystal the opportunity to say a final goodbye to her newborn daughter. Crying tears of hope and gratitude, Chrystal told little Hope that she'd done what she could to give her a chance at life. With the glowing eyes of a loving mother rather than a hopeless drug addict, she looked at the Holets and said, "Please love her and take care of her."

Hope is now one year old, and there have been many

*health struggles already in her young life. But Ryan would have
never thought of doing anything different. "These things don't
just happen. I was meant to meet Chrystal right at that precise
moment, and I was led to do something to help. We're cops;
that's what we do."*

Several aspects of a professional life of service are spiritual —
meaning selfless, purposeful, compassionate, loving. You're driven
by your heart to make a difference in your agency, with your colleagues, in the community, and for those you serve. This spiritual
component of service is essential for work to be meaningful, productive of wellness, and life affirming for you.

This inherent spiritual aspect of service is what enhances
resiliency, keeps you motivated, makes work more meaningful
and purposeful, and helps to keep you well and at peace. If you
want to make a difference, be nonviolent, compassionate, selfless, and giving in the totality of your being (thoughts, emotions,
speech, actions).

To make a difference you have to integrate yourself into the
reality that all life is connected, interrelated, and dependent upon
each other. Life is the energy of consciousness, and what you
think, feel, say, and do affects not only every aspect of your own
life, relationships, and wellness, but those of all others in your
sphere of influence as well.

Consciousness is fundamental, and the condition and right
use of your conscious awareness within this spirituality of service
will determine the quality of your service career, and the quality
of your life.

Consciousness can be defined as not just our mental abilities
and potential, but our awareness, our beliefs, our character, our
values, our instincts, our potential for doing good, our capacity to
love, our hopes, desires, and dreams. As science has been proving,

there is individual consciousness and a universal consciousness common to all human beings that connects us all.

Stephan A. Schwartz, research specialist in consciousness for over forty years and author of *The 8 Laws of Change* and *Opening to the Infinite*, asserts, with the backing of science, that all consciousness is (and therefore all people are) interrelated and interdependent. He has said, "People must open themselves to the idea that they are part of a great matrix of life and that the choices you make affect the shape and form that life will take for yourself, and everyone else affected by your thoughts, words, and actions."

Consciousness and spirituality are two sides of the same coin. And the spiritual elements of consciousness that consistently produce the most positive effects in our health and wellness are selflessness, generosity, love, compassion, kindness, understanding, humility, and gratitude. When these aspects of spiritual consciousness are cultivated and become consistently part of your service, you stand the greatest chance of not only maintaining but improving your health, wellness, and peace, as well as your influence with others.

The critical problem for first responders is that the everyday trauma of our professions erodes our ability to be consciously aware, purposeful, compassionate, and spiritual in our service. The trauma we experience can gradually, over time, suffocate our hearts. When the heart is suffocating one becomes uncaring, indifferent, disengaged with life, inactive, self-centered, less resilient, disinterested in trying to make a difference, and unhealthy. This is what makes so many first responders cynical, angry, frustrated, and unable to carry on close and meaningful relationships.

The good news is that you can reverse this negative force by proactively, consciously activating the tremendous healing capacity of your heart — purposefully putting your heart into your work, regardless of the outcomes. The essential principle to remember is to *consistently be driven by your heart to make the intentional, conscious effort to make a positive difference in all aspects of your service.* If you do this, your heart will respond and resist shutting down.

During a recent presentation of my emotional-survival and wellness training class, a probation officer from Northern California told me how she had become very disillusioned and indifferent after her failed efforts to help a juvenile offender. The seventeen-year-old male had been sent to juvenile hall for a series of robberies. This officer interacted with him numerous times every day over the nine months he was incarcerated.

The probation officer felt a connection to this young man and went out of her way every chance she had to speak with him, to offer advice and help, and to try to change his life. They had several very positive interactions. She was looking forward every morning to going back to interact with him.

Tragically, less than a month after his release from custody the juvenile was killed in a gang fight. Tears filled her eyes as she told me and the class this story and how it made her feel like nothing extra she did would ever make a difference — so why try anymore?

This is a critical concept to understand: The potential outcomes of our efforts of serving with a purposeful heart are extremely varied, and ultimately *do not matter.* We have absolutely no control over outcomes. We have influence during the moment at hand, and hopefully a lasting influence, but absolutely no control over the choices others make or the outcome of circumstances.

What's vital to understand is that our conscious intent and effort *at the time* we are serving with purposed compassion is what matters. In that effort, at that moment, we are doing something that can erase our past traumas, give us purpose, make us feel better, and enliven our spirit. During those nine months while she was giving herself in her service, that probation officer did make a difference both within herself and in unknown ways with the offender. That is what is healing, positive, and helpful. The fact that the juvenile decided to later disregard any good that was done and waste his life should not matter in the bigger picture of her efforts to make a difference.

It is *the conscious effort to do good and to make a difference in the present moment* that is essential. Also, if you never make the effort, then absolutely no added good will ever come to you or anyone else from your service.

Compassionate, Life Affirming, and Productive of Wellness

There is a part of us that is capable of transcending the self-centered, negative, instinctive aspect of human nature and transforming it into universal spiritual qualities such as selfless giving, love, compassion, service, and helpfulness. Purposed, spiritual consciousness in our service involves idealism and the great nobility of what it means to protect and serve.

First responders protect and give life to others, keep the peace, and prevent others from becoming victims of crime, natural disasters, and evil. Within this conscious awareness you have countless opportunities to positively influence others. Everything you think, say, and do affects not only yourself but also others in both positive and negative ways. The more spiritually conscious and aware you are, the more your influence will be positive, constructive, and helpful to others as well as to your own health and wellness.

Nearly every waking moment, we are constantly making choices, many without even thinking about them. The more you can become consciously aware of the choices you are making in even the small details of your life, the better your choices will be and the more influential you can be in creating positive change and making a meaningful difference.

No matter what choice you are about to make, there are always options; that's what makes it a choice. Among all our potential options, there will always be a choice that is more compassionate and life affirming, and therefore more productive of wellness, than all the others. Our affirmative efforts to promote wellness involve consistently and consciously striving to choose the most compassionate and life-affirming options available.

If you develop the ability to consistently make such choices, you will significantly enhance your health, wellness, and happiness; increase your resiliency, your sense of peace and fulfillment, your motivation, and your work satisfaction; and improve your survivability in your first-responder profession.

Compassionate

The one lesson I learned more than any other in nearly thirty years of police service is that police work (or any first-responder profession) is a vocation of the heart. If you are not driven by your heart to make a positive difference, then the job is going to eat you alive.

Being a police officer or other first responder boils down to the desire to serve, to help, to protect, to give of ourselves through caring and compassionate actions because people matter to us. It is a way of serving not only our country, but our community and our greater human family as well. Our service is an expression of love: love of country, love of peace and security, love of family and neighbors, love of our brother and sister human beings, and love of community.

Serving with compassion through acts of kindness, caring, and support means you are consciously trying to make a difference in every call, whether it is taking a petty theft report or investigating a violent rape or robbery; whether it is speaking with a colleague or interacting with a member of the community. Compassionate action is essential because that is what heals and feeds your heart, nourishes, inspires, and sustains it. That is what will keep you interested, engaged with life, able to relate to others in more meaningful ways, and increasingly able to not only survive but thrive in your career.

Compassion is the DNA of service. The first-responder professions are dedicated to relieving suffering, to serving the needs of others no matter who they may be, to standing up to evil, to solving problems, and to making a positive difference in people's lives. We don't always get the chance to save a life, but every day we get numerous opportunities to affect a life; and the more that we do so in purposeful and positive ways reflective of spiritual values, the more we are creating wellness within ourselves.

By serving with compassion and a purposeful heart, I in no way am implying that we should not arrest people or use reasonable force when needed. In my thirty-year police career there is nothing I loved more than arresting people. I was investigating crimes and arresting suspects even as a captain. I loved it because I knew that every arrest I made was saving unknown numbers of people from being a victim of a crime, because no one was being victimized by that suspect while he or she was in jail. I also realized that every arrest could potentially lead to an offender wanting to change their life.

We also of course need to use reasonable force to enforce the law and to protect ourselves and others. But we still treat people with dignity, try to always be fair and reasonable, and use the least amount of force necessary.

Serving with compassion means you are purposeful in promoting the greatest good; that you are trying to be helpful beyond what is needed just to handle the call for service. It means you are thoughtful, kind, considerate, understanding, tolerant, and selflessly helpful in any way you can be.

Compassionate service means trying to make that difference because you care about people, about the good you can potentially do; you care about the image of your agency, the professionalism of your service, your integrity and honor, and your influence to create positive change.

Serving with your heart and acting with compassion have many scientifically proven benefits. They include:

- reduced stress levels
- activation of the pleasure centers in your brain so you feel good
- increased resiliency and ability to cope
- positive mood
- increased motivation and job satisfaction
- enhanced overall mental and physical health
- lessened depression and anxiety
- increased ability to connect with and relate to others
- enhanced longevity and survivability

Being purposeful in serving with compassion to make a positive difference erases a lot of the negative influences of trauma and acute stress, protects the well-being that your job can erode if you're not careful, and increases your survivability, health, and wellness. Because all life is connected, what benefits others benefits you. When you are doing something good for another, you are in fact doing something good for yourself.

Life Affirming

For every choice we make each day, there is always an option that is more life affirming than the others. You will not be able to realize which option that is if you are not conscious about wanting to do more that is life affirming. By *life affirming* I mean choices that:

- will add to your peace rather than take away from it;
- will enhance your health and wellness rather than deplete them;
- will increase your joy and sense of fulfillment; and
- will add meaning or contribute to your experience in a positive, constructive way rather than being negative, hurtful, destructive, or useless.

In our day-to-day lives, many things do nothing to enhance our wellness, peace, and quality of life. Every choice we make needs to be both compassionate (to ourselves and to others) and life affirming. If your choice is not compassionate and life affirming, then it will be eroding your resiliency, eroding your motivation; depleting your energy, your enjoyment, your peace and wellness; and most significantly, eroding your ability to care and be useful. This of course leads to the potential cancers of first-responder professions: indifference, disengagement, carelessness, and disconnection from others.

Productive of Wellness

If everything you do is both compassionate and life affirming, then it will be productive of wellness. You cannot be well and resilient when you are not practicing the vital components that are essential for enhancing your health and well-being.

The habits, thought patterns, and negative beliefs that are so natural to many of us are slowly destroying our ability to create a foundation of inner wellness and peace. The instinctive dismissive ways we respond to certain persons; the negative emotions of anger, fear, resentment, and judgment; being unforgiving; thinking negatively; not being proactive about increasing our physical, mental, emotional, and spiritual wellness — all of these greatly diminish our capacity to thrive and survive in our profession.

The remedy to all of this is to *become more consciously aware and purposeful in our choices to be more compassionate and life affirming.* I know this is real and is tremendously effective, not only because I lived it and in many ways it saved my career and life, but because I've seen it work for countless others.

The undeniable secret to not only surviving a first-responder career but loving it and remaining healthy and well throughout your many years of service is to be driven by your spiritual heart to make a difference, to create positive change, to alleviate suffering, and to be useful to others. The surest way to increase your survivability, work through trauma, and enjoy a greater quality of life in your service career? Make compassion and life-affirming actions become as natural as breathing.

In his incredibly inspiring book *Man's Search for Meaning*, psychiatrist Viktor E. Frankl writes of his experiences in a Nazi concentration camp during World War II and the power that purposed compassion had in saving lives. He was kept in the concentration camp for three years and suffered immensely, nearly dying several times. Death, starvation, and cruelty beyond description were his and the other prisoners' reality in every moment.

Frankl writes that the prisoners who tended to survive were those few who found meaning and purpose even in their horrific suffering. The ones who usually survived were those who did things like give their one piece of daily bread to another prisoner starving more than they were. Their purposefulness in helping, their love for others, and their selfless giving sustained them even in the midst of terrible suffering.

According to Frankl, our emotional well-being depends on our ability to find meaning in our lives greater than the satisfaction of our instincts — greater than our self-interest. That is the key to surviving and thriving throughout your career of service.

The Spiritual Nature of Service

Thomas Jefferson beautifully expressed in our Declaration of Independence that all persons are created equal and are endowed by their creator with certain inalienable rights — life, liberty, and the pursuit of happiness. The United States is unique in the world in declaring that such rights are sacred and are given to all equally from God, which is why the Constitution enshrines the fundamental precept that no government can ever take them away without due process. The police and other first responders have been entrusted by the people to secure these God-given rights.

There is an inherent spirituality in service and in being responsible for the protection of life and our sacred rights. Such spirituality is expressed through our highest motives and selfless desire to go beyond our self-interests to give ourselves in the service of others, or, many of us would say, in the service of God.

I believe that as first responders dealing constantly with life, death, evil, and good, the concept of a universal presence of goodness or the guiding hand of God is often inescapable. Any spiritual practice or religious faith's main purpose is to bring people to a more perfect union with each other, and with God. Any such practice can not only be comforting and inspiring to a first responder but also offer support, guidance, understanding, purpose, healing, and peace. It can help you maintain a positive perspective in your work life and provide coping mechanisms to positively process emotional and psychological trauma. It offers a shield for your spirit.

If a particular faith or spiritual practice is or was once a part of your life, nurture it and use it for your well-being. The spiritual values of service (love, compassion, generosity, selflessness, connectedness, sacrifice, striving to do good and be a positive influence to help others) are inspired from a source beyond human intellect. They run contrary to a human being's selfish interests of mere survival. These are the very values that make life, and a life of service, meaningful. For many of us who serve, the wellspring of these spiritual values is a source that creates and gives life. And I believe that if we ignore that which gives life, our lives and service will be adversely affected in many ways.

Our inner spirit is the foundation of life, for it comprises our capacity to love, to be resilient, to cope, to do good, to live with integrity and character, to live our faith and beliefs, to keep a clean conscience, and to remain motivated. It is the foundation of our overall health and wellness.

Our inner spirit is assaulted constantly by the daily traumas we experience at work, and it is those spiritual values that restore, renew, inspire, and heal our inner spirit. The spiritual aspect of ourselves provides the foundation for a life of service. As Helen Keller once said, "The best and most beautiful things in the world cannot be seen or even touched, but just felt in the heart." Keeping this spiritual reality in mind will increase your odds of surviving and thriving as a first responder.

The Spiritual Elements of Service

The spiritual elements of our service include love, compassion, charity, generosity, gratitude, connectedness, right motivation (being selfless), integrity, and helpfulness. These aspects of service all enhance resiliency, increase peace, renew our energy, increase our sense of meaningful fulfillment, increase our joy, and enhance overall health.

The negative elements of human nature, which include envy, jealousy, unbridled ambition, pride, revenge, overbearing ego, selfishness, unforgiveness, expressing negativity, and anger, are all poisonous to our inner spirit and our ability to be well and to serve. The more you make the conscious effort to express the spiritual elements and transcend the negative ones, the healthier you will be and the more good you will be able to do. Remaining connected to the spiritual elements of service has been the single greatest influence that enabled me to work in law enforcement for thirty years while remaining healthy, positive, motivated, and at peace.

Coping with Victimization

For an emergency first responder it can be very difficult to deal with the suffering of others. First responders are always in the middle of heartache. These senseless tragedies, however, provide countless opportunities to try to make a difference by listening, offering hope, or filling a need. Sometimes all a first responder can do is listen, be compassionate, and find a few kind words that might offer hope.

It's always difficult seeing people suffer (if it's not, then you've been in this job too long without nurturing your emotional wellness). At times it's hard not to suffer with them. To avoid this pain, some of us fall into the trap of shutting down emotionally. In the process we lose some of ourselves and become emotionally calloused — not feeling things anymore and being indifferent, disengaged, and emotionally dead inside. Emotional apathy is very difficult to recover from, and it can affect every aspect of your personal life. Being so affected, you don't feel joy with your kids or close with your spouse. That's always a potential hazard of the job, given what you experience every day. In fact, one officer recently told me he has realized that he now has to make a conscious effort to be nice to his kids because it just doesn't come naturally anymore.

When you focus on the spiritual aspect of service, the more you try to help and do good where it matters, the less likely it is that you will be affected by such suffering. The more you look for opportunities to create positive change and to fill a need, the more resilience you will have.

Remembering the Positive Outcomes of Your Work

Over the years I've had people come into the police department and thank me for arresting them. Because of their arrest, they were finally able to get off drugs, or the shock of being arrested gave them the impetus to turn their life around. Those instances remind me of why we are so needed and all the potential good we can do with each encounter.

There is a fundamental principle regarding all the good you do and its long-lasting effects on your health and well-being: *focusing on the positive makes the negative lose its power.* Imagine a white-board that is divided in half. On the right side is a list of every bad experience you've had at work: a dead baby, a fight for your life, another act of violence, another child molestation, another tragic vehicle accident, and all the others. On the left side, envision a list of all the good things you have been able to do: sponsoring a child to play sports, adopting a poor family for Christmas, volunteering as a mentor, helping out an elderly couple, supporting a colleague, serving as a member of the peer-support team, and countless other self-initiated actions. Such voluntary actions do so much good for us and are of course in addition to all the positive, good things we do every day in protecting and serving others — things like providing medical aid, preventing a crime, arresting a drug dealer or gang member, solving a neighborhood dispute, protecting people's free speech and freedom to assemble peacefully, and so much more. Every good, positive item on the left automatically erases a lot of the bad experiences on the right.

That's just how the mind works. Good, selfless service to others erases a lot of your past traumas. I know it to be an absolute fact; I have lived it and seen it. Once you have finally reached retirement, you don't want to be spending your time trying to forget all the bad; spend it remembering all the good you were able to accomplish.

Several years ago, four men were going around the suburban San Diego area getting homeless men drunk and then having them fight each other for more beer. The result was a notorious and wildly popular set of videos known as "Bum Fights." The four men made hundreds of thousands of dollars selling these videos. The homeless men were often badly injured in the fights, including broken bones and concussions.

Everyone in the police department knew what was going on, but no one thought it was a crime. I looked into the matter and searched for something we could arrest the "filmmakers" for, since the homeless men were being cruelly victimized and seriously hurt — even hospitalized.

After researching the penal code, I was able to find an obscure crime no one had ever heard of before — *instigating two people to fight other than an authorized state prize fight.* This law, enacted in 1872, was intended primarily to prevent underground boxing matches. Since more than one filmmaker was involved and working together, it made the alleged crime a felony — conspiracy to conduct an unauthorized prize fight. After a four-month investigation, the filmmakers were arrested and charged. They were subsequently convicted.

Then a miracle occurred. One of the homeless men had been a chronic drunk since the age of twelve. He was in his late forties when "Bum Fights" started. When the organizers were arrested and prosecuted, a citizen came forward and took this homeless man under his care. He'd seen the homeless man in his neighborhood and was so moved by his plight that he took it upon himself to help out. As a result, the homeless man has now been clean and sober for the ensuing fifteen years. He has lectured on college campuses about homelessness and alcoholism and has even been to the state capitol to speak with legislators about these problems. His turnaround was the most dramatic I had seen in thirty years of law enforcement. Because we tried to make a difference, this man was given a new life and has himself helped many people.

The potential effects of being driven by your heart to make a difference through the inherent spirituality of service can be tremendous and far reaching. Strive to be purposeful in your service, consciously committed to always choosing to be both compassionate and life affirming, and your career will become productive of wellness.

> Spirituality reflects the most sophisticated mindset,
> and the most powerful force available for the
> transformation of human suffering.
>
> — **MARIANNE WILLIAMSON**

Prayer of the Emergency First Responder

Living Spirit of all life, love, and compassion:
Guide me to selflessly serve those who need me;
Lead me to go and be where I can be of most use and do the most good;
Help me to bring justice and peace to those who have suffered;
Enable me to protect and give life with mercy;
Sustain and protect my spirit, that I will be inspired with greater purpose;
Protect me from the evil of others;
Nurture and heal my soul, that I will not suffer from what I see;
Help me to serve this day with compassion, integrity, and mercy;
Give me the inner strength to endure heartache, pain, and frustration;
Comfort my spirit that whatever I may face this day, I will forever remain at peace.

Self-Awareness Questions: The Spirituality of Service

As we look within ourselves to discover ways of being more useful and helpful to others, our agency, and the community, we experience greater purpose, motivation, peace, resiliency, and wellness. The following questions are meant to assist you in finding a more spiritual purpose in your service.

How compassionate and life affirming are your choices and your service?

In what ways can you be more purposeful in serving with your heart and trying to make a difference?

What positive change can you make in your agency, with your colleagues, and in the community you serve?

What specific things can you do to practice the spiritual elements of service in being more loving, more selfless, more understanding, more compassionate?

Chapter Seven

BRAIN INJURIES
CAUSED BY TRAUMA

PTSD and Ways to Heal

We must accept finite disappointment,
but never lose infinite hope.
— Martin Luther King Jr.

Officer Taylor called in sick for the fifth day in a row. She hadn't gotten out of bed in those five days other than to go to the bathroom or to scrounge up something to eat. She lay in bed staring outside as the world went by, oblivious to the emotional pain she was trying to endure.

Taylor had once been an enthusiastic officer who loved going to work every day. Now, eight years later, she didn't understand what had happened to her. She couldn't remember the last time she really enjoyed anything. She was unable to connect with her family and now avoided her friends, fearing they would think she was losing her mind. She hated the thought of going in to work.

Officer Taylor had become calloused, unable to feel anything for anyone. The only thing she felt now was the emptiness and helplessness inside her. The pain in her spirit was overpowering and absolute; it felt like a sword had pierced her soul. Her heart ached beyond description. She felt hopeless, unable to cope with the prospect of continuing on in her depression.

That's when Taylor saw her service handgun on the counter in the other room. She realized that the only way she could end her emotional suffering was to end her life. She walked over to the counter and stared at her gun belt. As she slowly wrapped her trembling fingers around the butt of her handgun, she felt some comfort. That weapon had kept her safe for eight years; now it would give her peace. She set down the handgun and walked back to her bed, passing a photo in the hallway of herself smiling as an officer newly graduated from the police academy.

Taylor sat in bed, holding the gun in her right hand and resting it on her lap. Tears began to roll down her cheeks as she lifted the barrel of the gun toward her open mouth. At that moment, her cat jumped up on the bed, purring and rubbing his face against her thigh. Taylor had the immediate thought that after she killed herself, no one would take care of her cat. Her love for her cat caused her to come out of her trance and begin thinking about how she might keep living. She was able to pull herself together and seek the help she needed through the police psychologist and the peer-support team. She had had no idea that she'd been suffering from intense PTSD, and she soon realized she wasn't losing her mind but had suffered a serious injury to her mind and spirit. After only a few sessions of an extremely effective treatment for PTSD called EMDR (eye movement desensitization and reprocessing), she began to recover. Officer Taylor is now doing well.

Because a career as an emergency first responder inherently exposes us to repeated and significant traumatic incidents and acute stress, it is impossible for us to avoid events that can cause PTSD. Every day we experience trauma, which is defined as any experience that has the potential to negatively affect us over a long period of time. Some traumas are severe, while others are less so. All trauma is caustic to our brain and central nervous system, as well as cumulative. Trauma eats away at our resiliency, peace, health, and well-being. For this reason, it's essential for you to learn how to prepare yourself to constructively process the repeated trauma of your profession.

It is estimated that hundreds of thousands of current and former emergency first responders are suffering from PTSD, anywhere from 20 to 30 percent. Just one major traumatic incident or the cumulative effects of repeated traumatic situations can develop into PTSD, which is actually an injury to the brain's ability to process a critical incident or acute stress, and may result in several seriously debilitating symptoms. And trauma can not only injure your brain; it can kill you through suicide.

PTSD is brought about by continued exposure to tragedies, extremely disturbing experiences, or psychological trauma causing intense fear, horror, or helplessness. Death, the suffering of others, violence, injuries, suicides, child molestation and abuse, dangers, and threats are all forms of trauma that can alter how our brain functions. Every emergency first responder is susceptible to these potentially debilitating injuries to the mind and spirit, but there are ways to prepare for and process trauma that can significantly reduce the intensity and duration of symptoms.

PTSD Symptoms and How They Develop

It is important to understand the development of PTSD from a psychological perspective. PTSD tends to develop after a critical incident in which an emergency first responder has been exposed to trauma that concerned actual or threatened death or grave harm. It can also develop over time, after a person has endured repeated, significantly stressful and intensely dangerous situations or a variety of other traumas that we experience nearly every day, with lingering effects. The typical emotions experienced during such incidents include extreme fear, helplessness, shock, disgust, and alarm. During or after the incident, you may experience emotional numbing, the inability to recall information or details related to the incident, the feeling of being in a fog, depression, and a repeated sense of watching yourself from a distance.

Well after the incident is over, PTSD sufferers may reexperience the trauma through flashbacks, night terrors, or illusions — seeing things that are not real or are not happening, yet are experienced as real. Physical symptoms of PTSD may include an extremely heightened sense of hypervigilance along with an inability to relax, extreme anxiety, serious difficulty sleeping, and intense agitation. You may also try to avoid any reminder of the critical incident by staying clear of certain people or locations, switching your shift, or not coming to work. You may even experience inadvertent incidents of dereliction of duty. Other potential symptoms include significant mood disturbances, which may result in feeling disconnected from others and an inability to express feelings in the way you did previously, or having wide-ranging emotions that you have never experienced before that seemingly come from nowhere. The emergency first responder suffering from PTSD may also experience intrusive thoughts, angry rages, the inability to concentrate or focus, an exaggerated startle response, continued depression, uncontrollable emotions, and the inability to stop mentally replaying the traumatic event over and over again.

These symptoms tend to have a profound negative effect on work performance and one's overall quality of life. They often lead to poor coping skills or to risk-taking behaviors, such as excessive drinking, drug use (legal and illegal), promiscuity and affairs, and various addictions, such as gambling, pornography, and others. Other signs of maladaptive coping include difficulties in family relationships and an excessive desire to isolate yourself.

It is key for you to realize that *all these symptoms are a natural, normal physiological reaction as the mind attempts to process trauma*, since the brain's normal processing ability has been injured. You may experience these symptoms to a greater or lesser degree than someone else, but every emergency first responder is susceptible to undergoing a PTSD injury and symptoms. The most important thing for you to remember is that if you are experiencing any of these symptoms, it is critical to seek help. Symptoms will not just go away with time without an intervention of trauma therapy such as EMDR or others (discussed later).

Struggling to resist or hide the symptoms can inadvertently cause symptoms to worsen and become seriously life altering. These symptoms do not typically just suddenly go away. You need to be trained in advance to deal with them, or helped through the experience. That way, your mind can positively and effectively place the traumatic event in the proper perspective and, by doing so, alleviate the symptoms and release the trauma from your brain and central nervous system.

There is never any shame in needing or seeking help; it is normal. In fact, as a matter of emotional survival and wellness, you should see a certified trauma therapist annually who is experienced in PTSD and in treating first responders as part of a regular pattern of prevention and wellness maintenance — even if you are not experiencing any symptoms. The only shame is not doing everything you can to be well; to enjoy life, family, and work; and to move forward. It would be a tragedy to choose to suffer through something that reduces the quality of your life when there is assistance available that has been proven effective. PTSD is not about what's wrong with you — it is about what *happened* to you, and it can be healed.

The effects of trauma and PTSD symptoms can be not only terrifying but crippling. Those suffering can often feel hopeless, fearful, unable to function or to be normal in their daily routines. A good pointer to remember while you are struggling and getting help is to focus on doing the next right thing, or the next helpful thing, to get you through the day. It is helpful to ask yourself several times throughout the day, "What is the next right thing I can do?" For some struggling, the next right thing might be just to get out of bed. Then the next right thing may be to take a shower, to eat — just simple things to help keep you active, involved, and moving forward.

Preparation: The Key to Mitigating the Effects of PTSD

To increase resiliency, limit the intensity of PTSD symptoms, and constructively process trauma, preparation is critical. You will need to be both mentally and physically prepared in order to provide yourself with the best chance for surviving emotionally. In addition to the spiritual wellness practices described in chapter 2 — which inherently fortify the mind, spirit, and emotions, enabling them to deal with a traumatic incident once it happens — the following wellness methods, too, will assist you in preparing for and mitigating the effects of trauma.

Set Up a Support System

Develop a trusted support system made up of family and friends. Discuss with them what to expect, how you are likely to behave after a critical incident — either after a traumatic event or after consistent exposures to significant stress — and how they can best support and most effectively help you. Remember, your physical, mental, and emotional health and well-being, as well as the quality of your life, all depend on your level of preparedness and the development of an effective support system. Tell the people closest to you what you need from them.

Get an Annual Emotional-Survival and Wellness Checkup

As a form of prevention and wellness maintenance, consult with a psychologist specializing in treating emergency first responders and trauma to determine if you are being adversely affected by past trauma and to gain insight into how to deal with trauma and stress more effectively.

The idea behind an annual checkup like this is *not* that "something is wrong." Something may or may not be affecting you, but the emphasis is on getting a wellness check and discussing the previous year — both professionally and personally — regardless, as a preventative and wellness-maintenance measure. This is similar as going to a physician each year for a physical checkup. The goal is to accomplish several different things:

1. Discuss issues that are currently concerning you; talk about how things have gone professionally and personally over the preceding year.
2. Explore the past year in general and look for areas of concern or in which you might wish to make changes.
3. Examine the coping skills and resiliency you have exhibited during previous stressful and traumatic events. Discuss what your coping mechanisms are. Are they healthy? How might you improve on them?
4. Set goals for the next year.
5. Become comfortable talking with a therapist who is an expert in dealing with trauma, PTSD, and first responders. That way, you'll be more comfortable seeking assistance if you ever feel it is needed in the future.

Mentally Rehearse to Prepare Yourself

Work at developing a mindset that recognizes that you may very well eventually experience a significant traumatic incident, and that you will survive. Envision how you will handle such an experience both during and after the fact, and what would help you process the trauma and place it in its proper perspective. Mental rehearsal and visualization — seeing yourself experience a traumatic incident and coming through it all right — is essential. It is also important to realize that you do not have to ever be involved in a major critical incident to suffer from PTSD. Most first responders with PTSD got it from the daily, smaller traumas that we are constantly exposed to.

Practice Tactical Breathing

According to Lt. Col. David Grossman (coauthor of *Warrior Mindset* and *On Combat*), tactical breathing has been shown to dramatically help people not only function at the highest levels during a traumatic event but also cope with the aftermath. Essentially, tactical breathing consists of the following: Just before or after a traumatic incident, or while your mind is reliving the event, take a big breath in through your nose, hold it, then breathe out of your mouth slowly for four seconds. Then repeat this several times. This will calm and center the automatic responses of your mind and body to stress.

Do Critical-Incident Stress Management (CISM) Debriefing or Defusing

Participate in a critical-incident stress management debriefing or defusing within a few days of experiencing a critical incident. (These debriefings and defusings are explained later in this chapter.)

Don't Postpone Professional Assistance

Shortly after a serious critical incident, seek assistance from a psychologist who has experience in traumatic events, whether you think you need it or not. Most agencies have a contract with such psychologists (through the Employee Assistance Program) and offer a certain number of confidential visits for free or at a significantly reduced cost. Treatments for PTSD can be relatively short-term and extremely effective, especially if sought soon after an incident. It is never too late to seek help and to have your traumatically injured brain healed.

Keep Yourself Well Hydrated

Develop the habit of consistently being well hydrated — with water, not energy drinks, coffee, or sports drinks. Maintaining good hydration helps the brain remain alert and able to process trauma more effectively. Good hydration coupled with good sleep management will significantly help you be prepared for trauma and will lessen its effects.

Discuss the Incident

Find understanding people to talk with who will listen without judgment. Peer-support colleagues (see chapter 9) who have experienced traumatic events offer an invaluable, confidential, and trusted resource; they are individuals you can talk with in order to begin to process the trauma.

After the Injury: Symptoms and Treatments

PTSD is a complex injury to the brain's coping ability in which the affected person's memory, emotional responses, intellectual processes, and nervous system have all been disrupted. PTSD can occur immediately or weeks or years after a traumatic critical incident or an accumulation of incidents. Approximately 40 percent of those experiencing PTSD symptoms have a delayed onset of symptoms; about 80 percent of people who develop PTSD also develop other serious health issues, such as heart disease, diabetes, and excessive weight gain.

There are several signs that you and your family members should look for that potentially signal the development of PTSD. These signs include the following:

- broken sleep because of nightmares or night terrors
- outbursts of anger over insignificant things or things that normally would never bother you
- withdrawing from interaction with family, friends, and activities
- having difficulty at work
- taking more leave from work than normal
- drinking too much or abusing medications in order to sleep or forget
- becoming anxious, and possibly even vomiting, before going to work

Many times a person suffering from PTSD does not realize what has happened or how they have changed. If family members or coworkers see some of these signs, it is critical for them to ask questions and offer help. Coworkers and family can assist the person in seeking help in a positive way, by supporting and showing genuine concern for the affected person's well-being without judging, criticizing, or pressuring the person to just "get over it."

The following nonintrusive, nonjudgmental questions can be used to begin a conversation:

- "The other day I noticed that you weren't really yourself. Has anything been bothering you?"

- "Do you want to get some coffee to catch up? I've noticed over the past few weeks that you haven't been yourself."
- "I'm concerned about you — how are you doing? If you ever need to talk or need anything at all, I'm here for you."

See chapter 10 for detailed information on what a spouse or other family members can do to support their emergency first responder.

There are several effective treatments for PTSD, such as cognitive behavioral therapy, cognitive processing therapy, prolonged exposure therapy, stress inoculation therapy, and EMDR. All of these are endorsed by the Department of Defense, the Department of Veterans Affairs, the American Psychiatric Association, and the International Society for Traumatic Stress Studies. The rest of this chapter covers two tools that many first responders find especially effective.

Eye Movement Desensitization and Reprocessing (EMDR) Therapy

One of the most effective treatments is EMDR. The theory behind it is that traumatic experiences upset the biochemical balance of the brain. EMDR is a form of accelerated information processing that tends to unblock the brain's information-processing system. EMDR seems to allow the brain to complete the processing that was left unfinished after the traumatic event, when the brain's normal processing was altered as a result of the traumatic incident or cumulative incidents.

I have had EMDR therapy, and something that had bothered me off and on for twenty-five years went away after one session. I could not recommend it strongly enough. It is extremely effective. More likely than not, you will experience some or complete relief of your symptoms after only a few sessions. In my travels around the country teaching, I have never heard one negative thing about

EMDR. What I typically hear is "It's the best thing that ever happened to me. I should have done it years ago. It saved my life."

This most effective therapy can be exhausting and emotionally draining in the short term, but overall it's a relatively easy process by which many or all of the negative, dark emotions and thoughts associated with your memories of trauma become disassociated and released. You still remember the incidents, but they no longer adversely affect you. The healing effects are permanent.

The purpose of EMDR is to enable a mental restructuring of information about the traumatic event that has not been resolved and normally processed. It helps eliminate the surge of emotion that an individual experiences when thinking about or talking about the event. Traumas that have not been mentally resolved are associated with negative perspectives on issues of self-control, which relate to the negative images manifesting themselves in many forms throughout a person's life.

Traumatic events that have been completely processed and resolved by means of EMDR appear to accelerate the process necessary to allow assimilation of the trauma into previously held views and norms.

Using a three-pronged approach, the therapist addresses the original traumatic incident, elicits the present internal and environmental triggers that stimulate poorly adaptive behavior, and installs a desired behavioral response that then becomes natural. The following story, written by a fire captain from an agency in Southern California, is a great example of how effective EMDR can be.

As a fire captain, I, along with my colleagues, have responded to hundreds of auto accidents, including many disturbing fatalities. One crash initially seemed like all the rest. An innocent victim, no known name, only the unmistakable image of a lifeless face staring into the far-off distance. A drunk driver had killed this twenty-six-year-old woman, who had been doing the right thing by acting as the designated driver for her husband on the ride home in the early morning hours.

The scene was as routine as a DUI crash can be: two bloodied bodies lying in spinal stabilization before being loaded into a single ambulance heading to the hospital. One of them was just hearing the news that his young wife was dead, as the other was being informed that he had just killed a woman. Meanwhile, the victim still lay covered on the roadway, her bloodied body staining the sheet, a lifeless corpse who had been a vibrant and beautiful young woman only minutes earlier.

Unfortunately, the scene of mangled vehicles and scattered debris was routine to us. The same old story of tragedy and unnecessary death. But for some reason, this particular young woman's face was burned into my brain. I couldn't stop seeing that lifeless face with her wide-open eyes looking right through me. It wasn't completely out of the ordinary for images of disturbing scenes and tragedy to trouble me for the remainder of a shift. But this incident was different, a totally new and unwelcome experience.

I kept seeing the dead woman's face — night after night, day after day. There were times I looked at my wife and saw the dead girl gazing back at me. I had a good support system at home, which is crucial, as well as at work; but because I didn't even know I had a problem, I couldn't use the support I had in place.

My wake-up call was a terrifying dream I had about a week after the incident. I dreamed that I was back at the scene, smelling leaking gasoline, stepping over tangled debris, while attempting to remove the young woman from the car as a body recovery. In the dream, as had happened in real life, the young woman was obviously dead, with severe trauma to her head.

But in the dream, as I grabbed her upper body in an attempt to lift her out of the tangled wreckage, she abruptly opened her eyes and told us that we killed her. I snapped out of my sleep in a cold sweat, trembling. I knew it was time to seek help. I didn't know what was going on with me, and I wondered if I was starting to lose my mind.

Help came initially from my fire department through the Employee Assistance Program, which set me up with a therapist. Ultimately, this resulted in a treatment that I had never heard of, called EMDR. I was more than willing to try anything that might get these visions and dreams out of my head. Nothing I had tried on my own was working. The more I tried to forget, the clearer the disturbing images became and the more frequently they showed up.

Incredibly, one treatment was all it took as I embraced the process with metaphorical open arms. It was an amazing transformation as I "saw" the treatment work in my own mind and actually found closure to this event. To this day I have no idea why this particular incident had such a dramatic impact on me. I don't know why I needed treatment for this call more than any other, but I'm thankful that I found it.

To find a certified EMDR therapist in your area, visit the EMDR International Association website: www.emdria.org.

Critical-Incident Stress Management

Critical-incident stress management (CISM) is a proactive, comprehensive approach to mitigating the effects of a potentially debilitating critical incident. It encompasses both prevention and intervention. Prevention involves equipping people with resources before an actual crisis so that they can potentially cope better or even avert the development of PTSD symptoms. Continued, periodic training is also a component of CISM. This provides education regarding the nature of critical-incident stress, basic stress management strategic coping skills, and resiliency. Establishing realistic expectations regarding the nature of stress reactions can be crucial in combating misconceptions of invulnerability.

CISM Debriefings

Studies and personal experience have shown that a professional and proper CISM debriefing (typically held one to three days after the event) of people involved in any serious traumatic incident can be extremely beneficial. A CISM debriefing is a structured group discussion with all persons involved in the traumatic incident, including dispatchers and call takers. The structured discussion lasts two to three hours and is facilitated by a mental health practitioner experienced with trauma using the CISM model developed by J. T. Mitchell. There are modified versions of the Mitchell model that are equally effective.

The CISM debriefing is also attended by peer-support team members and, ideally, a department chaplain. Attendance at the facilitated discussion is mandatory for those involved in a traumatic incident, but participants speak voluntarily. Nancy Bohl-Penrod, director of the Counseling Team International (https://the counselingteam.com), has slightly modified the standard seven-phase Mitchell model of CISM to include nine phases. The debriefing allows for both mental and emotional processing of thoughts, feelings, and reactions. It also provides information on stress management and coping strategies. Reasons for a CISM debriefing and its therapeutic effects include the following:

1. *Early intervention.* Early counseling prevents the crystallization of traumatic memories.
2. *Opportunity to verbalize the trauma.* Verbally reconstructing and expressing specific traumas, fears, and regrets leads to reduced stress reactions and symptoms and can promote the constructive processing of trauma.
3. *Group support.* The group experience provides numerous healing factors that are intrinsic to the group process, including the validation of thoughts, emotions, and stress reactions.
4. *Peer support.* Peers can most effectively eradicate the myth that what the traumatized person is experiencing is unique, and they can suggest more appropriate stress-management techniques.
5. *Stress education.* This allows for a better understanding of the skills that can be learned in order to cope with stressful situations.
6. *Follow-up support.* People in need of further care can be more readily identified during follow-up sessions.

Example of a CISM Debriefing

In a typical CISM debriefing, the facilitator, the peer-support team members, and the chaplain begin by explaining the process and their roles, and clearing up any initial concerns of those present. The fact phase is next, in which participants describe, from their own perspectives, their involvement in the incident.

The fact phase is followed by the thought phase, in which participants talk about their thoughts associated with the critical incident and immediately afterward. During the reaction phase, participants are encouraged to express any emotions regarding the incident. This phase allows everyone to identify what was, for them, the most traumatic aspect of the incident, along with their associated emotional reactions to the trauma. This is followed by the symptoms phase, in which participants describe any stress-related symptoms experienced since the traumatic event. It also allows an opportunity for peers to validate those symptoms.

The unfinished-business phase allows participants to bring up anything from the present critical incident that reminds them of a past traumatic experience that may still be bothering them. Often, traumatic incidents resurrect memories of and intense emotions related to past traumatic experiences that have never been effectively processed. One such example is an instance when an officer described feeling and thinking he was going to die during the fatal shooting of a suspect. He mentioned that this incident didn't bother him nearly as much as an incident two years earlier, in which he was suddenly surprised by a man who shoved a loaded gun in his face and the officer had to react with his bare hands to defend himself. This phase was an ideal time for the facilitator to discuss and help the officer process that previous incident.

The goal of the teaching/educational phase is to educate the participants about critical-incident stress and coping tactics, possible symptoms that may be experienced after a delayed onset, and ways to mitigate those potential symptoms. This is followed by the wrap-up phase, in which participants can ask questions. Finally, in the round-robin/reentry phase, the facilitator clarifies any ambiguities, answers final questions, and makes summary statements that return the group to its normal mode of functioning.

CISM debriefings have proven to be highly effective when conducted properly — when no judgments or criticisms are made, no one is made to talk, and everyone who wants to speak is allowed to. For the more serious incidents, a secondary CISM debriefing is recommended. The life partners of the first responders who were involved attend this one, without the first responders being present. This meeting provides the family members with invaluable insights, support, and assistance so that they can most effectively support and care for their first-responder mates.

CISM Defusings

In contrast to a CISM debriefing, a defusing is a group discussion with all employees who were involved in the incident, usually within hours, which allows for an initial processing of the event and a discussion of the participants' immediate reactions to it. Typically a defusing involves peer-support team members only, without participation of a mental health practitioner. A defusing is informal, a shorter discussion for less serious incidents, but it still addresses the potential for participants to develop debilitating stress reactions. Defusings provide information about coping with stress, normalizing reactions, and assessing potential wellness needs.

Additional information and resources for treating PTSD are available from the National Center for PTSD at www.ptsd.va.gov, as well as from the Counseling Team International at https://the counselingteam.com.

Self-Awareness Questions for Dealing with Problems

List the reasons why you would not seek help to heal if you were suffering from PTSD symptoms. Then list all the reasons why you would seek help to heal. Which are more important to you?

Remember, trauma can not just injure your brain; it can kill you. Take it seriously. We deal with trauma every day at work. Become more aware of PTSD symptoms and tell someone if something is going on inside that you do not like.

In what ways do you cope with problems, and what can you do to more wisely and positively deal with them? Do you tend to ignore issues and feelings, or do you handle issues in a positive way as they arise?

Most people tend not to deal with their problems; they simply ignore them. As a first responder, you will find that this can become detrimental to your wellness and your coping ability. It's imperative to recognize issues and deal with them immediately in a positive, constructive way. Ignored feelings will only intensify. Simply recognizing them and becoming more aware of how they affect you is an important first step.

What gives you hope and why?

When you lose hope, you have nothing. It's vital to evaluate all the ways you are inspired, motivated, and encouraged and the reasons why those things give you hope. The more you cultivate hope, motivation, and inspiration, the more resilient you will become.

Chapter Eight

BᴇSTOW PHILOSOPHY

Beyond Survival
Toward Officer Wellness

The ultimate value of life depends upon awareness and the power
of contemplation rather than upon mere survival.

— **ARISTOTLE**

*Laura-Lee has worked as an emergency-room trauma nurse
for the past fourteen years. She has seen more people die, more
self-inflicted trauma, and more victims of senseless violence
than she could ever count. Through the years she developed her
own way of dealing with the suffering of others — she became
disconnected from them, as if they weren't really even people.
She tried to focus merely on the mechanics of her job. If someone died, it was just another body, not a person.*

*At times Laura-Lee had seen her fellow nurses look worse
than the patients: troubled, heartbroken, and helpless. She
promised herself that she would never be like that. But no
matter how hard she tried to function like a robot at work, she
couldn't fool her spirit. She learned this the hard way one night
when two small boys were rushed into the emergency room.*

A two-year-old and his four-year-old brother were brought in by paramedics, who were in the process of performing cardiopulmonary resuscitation (CPR) on both of them. While their mother was passed out drunk inside the house, the unattended boys had fallen into the swimming pool and drowned. The first medics who arrived dove into the pool to recover the boys lying at the bottom of the deep end.

Laura-Lee did her job and assisted as best she could. The boys' eyes were wide open, their lifeless bodies a dark blue. They were not breathing, and after a few more minutes of CPR they were declared dead. Laura-Lee had spent the afternoon lounging around her own pool at home, swimming and playing with her five-year-old son. As she looked at the small dead bodies, all she could see was her son's face. She told a colleague she wanted to take a short break and then walked into a bathroom, where she collapsed and cried hysterically. It was as if all the emotions she'd hidden away during the past fourteen years came up from deep within her at once. A coworker heard her crying uncontrollably and came to help her, but Laura-Lee was too distraught to continue working that evening.

Later, Laura-Lee began questioning whether she could do her job anymore. She became despondent over time, unable to sleep, and unable to get the faces of those two little dead boys out of her mind. She thought she was going crazy — nothing had ever affected her before. She felt lost, out of control, and filled with self-doubt.

Her emotions began to affect Laura-Lee's work, and for the first time in her career she was disciplined — twice in two weeks, for dereliction of duty. A hospital administrator who had known and worked with Laura-Lee for several years took her aside and asked what was going on with her. That conversation ultimately led the administrator to develop a wellness program for all hospital employees in order to address their emotional-survival and wellness needs.

Beyond Survival Toward Officer Wellness (BeSTOW) is a philosophy that derives from the fact that it is clearly not sufficient to merely train first responders to be physically safe so they can go home each night alive. It is also critical to develop proactive training so that first responders will be mentally, emotionally, and spiritually well, too. Developing and sustaining a vibrant and healthy spirit is more critical than any other form of training.

The BeSTOW philosophy should become ingrained in the culture of every first-responder agency by means of a wellness program for emotional survival. To create such a program, an appointed wellness program coordinator works with a team of employee volunteers committed to the wellness and healing of their colleagues. The BeSTOW philosophy is essential, and it can be equally effective in all first-responder professions.

The BeSTOW philosophy is based on research initiated by the Federal Bureau of Investigation. In 2008 the FBI's National Academy in Quantico, Virginia, began offering "Spirituality, Wellness, and Vitality Issues in Law Enforcement Practices," a course developed by Samuel Feemster, a supervising special agent in the bureau's Behavioral Science Unit. The course's core elements are relevant to all first responders. (Samuel Feemster has since retired and is now co-owner of Feemster Linkins Consulting. Along with Julie R. Linkins, he operates 911SALT.com, an organization dedicated to offering emotional- and spiritual-survival training and resources to first-responder agencies around the nation.)

The National Academy is a management academy for top law-enforcement officials all over the country and throughout the world. Each year, a thousand senior management officials attend the ten-week National Academy, of which I was a graduate in 2010.

The emphasis of BeSTOW training is on learning best practices for effectively processing emotional trauma and acute stress in order to keep first responders motivated and resilient, to prevent suicide, and to enhance wellness and survivability. The training focuses on effectively managing stress; constructively processing trauma and critical incidents; preparing for a critical incident; constructively dealing with first responders' own frustration, anger, and feelings of helplessness, and with others' ingratitude; and ways to prevent the numerous negative aspects of the job from depleting first responders' spirits and sense of purpose in serving.

Setting Up an Agency Wellness Program

The essential, minimum components of an effective wellness program based on the BeSTOW philosophy include the following:

The BeSTOW Team

This is the proactive component of a wellness program, and it consists of respected agency personnel from various divisions and units throughout the agency (sworn and nonsworn). These people actively develop and provide proactive training in emotional- and spiritual-survival and wellness practices.

The Peer-Support Team

Composed of devoted, trusted, and experienced colleagues, the peer-support team provides assistance and support in any form needed, including critical-incident stress management training, resources, and debriefings of agency employees. This support is provided to first responders who have experienced a critical incident or whose professional or personal lives are in need of support. Any first responder involved in a critical incident or experience who could potentially become significantly emotionally disturbed by it should be debriefed by the peer-support team.

A peer-support team is primarily reactive, responding to employees who have already suffered a traumatic event or a personal or professional crisis. Research has shown that emergency first responders are far more likely to talk with their peers than to seek help elsewhere. All communications with peer-support team members are strictly confidential, other than specific details included in mandated reports required by state laws. An agency may elect to combine the functions of the peer-support team and the BeSTOW team into one team that serves both purposes. More information on the peer-support team's functions and how to form a team are supplied in chapter 9. The following story demonstrates the impact a peer-support team can have.

La Mesa police officer Chris Rath was only the third woman ever hired as a police officer in La Mesa. Her small stature belied a tenacious spirit that endeared her to her male colleagues. Chris was an extremely conscientious officer who was totally devoted to her work. After serving for twenty-two years, she was looking forward to retiring in another eleven months. She and her sister owned and lived in a home that they had been remodeling, and Chris was active in horseback riding and caring for animals.

On September 3, 2002, Chris was diagnosed with pancreatic cancer at the age of fifty-two. She would be dead within six months. Frantically, Chris began trying to take care of everything that she wanted to do and felt needed to be done, for the sake of putting things in order before her death. Unfortunately, with her strength rapidly declining, she soon was unable to do much of anything.

The two sisters' home was in disarray at the time of Chris's diagnosis, with several major renovations and projects only partly completed. Chris felt terrible about having to leave such disorder for her sister to deal with alone.

The La Mesa Police Department peer-support team was made up of Chris's colleagues — officers and civilian staff of the police department who were devoted to caring for and assisting employees in need. Shortly after Chris's diagnosis, members of the team began to consistently call her, visit her, run errands for her, and do everything they could to care for her.

The team also formed a three-day work party and completely finished all the work on the property that the sisters had begun, including tiling the floors, purchasing a new stove and dishwasher, replacing fixtures in bathrooms, repairing a dilapidated patio, and clearing an acre and a half of brush. Throughout her illness, team members brought Chris food and flowers and spent time talking with her.

During the last two weeks of her life, two peer-support team members took turns staying with her day and night and helped her mother through the turmoil of watching her daughter slowly die. They were there with Chris and her family when she died. The family later sent the team a letter telling them how much all the visits and support had meant to Chris. They also wrote that they had been overwhelmed by how caring the officers and department employees had been, and that they could never express all the gratitude they felt.

Employee Assistance Program (EAP)

This program offers confidential professional counseling services that are contracted by the governing authority or agency. It allows employees to confidentially seek counseling services free of charge for a limited number of visits. After that, employees can usually continue to receive the same services but at a reduced rate. Confidential access to professional services such as these is critical for the well-being of first responders. Contracted within an EAP program should be one or more certified trauma therapists with experience treating first responders for PTSD.

Chaplain Program

It is important for any first-responder agency to have an active chaplain program that is engaged with and effective at providing emotional and spiritual comfort and support to first responders, as well as free and legally protected counseling when requested. Details and examples of an effective chaplain program, and how to form one, are discussed in chapter 11.

Physical Fitness Standards and Program

Policies, standards, and programs that promote the physical health of employees are essential to maintaining overall wellness, and first-responder agencies must develop and support them. The La Mesa Police Department has a voluntary physical fitness program in which, once per quarter, employees can test themselves and be awarded points based on their physical condition. Those who earn a high enough number of points receive up to one additional week of vacation time each year.

Initiating the BeSTOW Philosophy in a Wellness Program

In order for the BeSTOW philosophy to work effectively in an agency or organization, it must be embraced and supported by those in upper management. However, the training initiatives and impetus should come from line-level, or nonsupervisory, personnel to create acceptance of the program.

To form a BeSTOW team, the wellness coordinator should select employees who are well respected throughout the agency and who demonstrate a passion for supporting emotional survival. The team will be most effective if team members serve on a voluntary basis, so that only those truly interested will get involved with it.

Initially, a written statement defining the team's mission and purpose will need to be developed. A department instruction or general order should be written to provide guidelines for the work of the BeSTOW team. (If you wish to receive examples of such guidelines, email me at dwillis1121@yahoo.com.) The team should plan to meet at regular intervals, on an ongoing basis, to develop a process for training others in the BeSTOW philosophy.

Part of learning how to develop emotional-survival training is to receive training yourself. Books like *Emotional Survival for Law Enforcement* by Kevin Gilmartin, *The Body Keeps the Score: Brain, Mind, and Body in the Healing of Trauma* by Bessel van der Kolk, and *Force under Pressure: How Cops Live and Why They Die* by Lawrence Blum are excellent starting points. Additionally, an agency can seek help in this from one of several trainers who travel to provide such training. I am one of those trainers, and Clarke Paris, Kevin Gilmartin, Lt. Col. David Grossman, Sam Feemster, Blue Courage (https://bluecourage.com), and 1st Responder Conferences (https://1stresponderconferences.org), among others, also offer this service.

The BeSTOW team should use a well-thought-out method for introducing the philosophy and training to members of the agency. I have found it most effective to initially discuss how the job has adversely affected us, and then to ask what we can do to mitigate those effects in order to protect ourselves. This introduction should entail a description of what BeSTOW is *not*.

BeSTOW is not religion, and it is not people talking about their feelings or sitting around holding each other. It does not force anyone to talk about something they do not want to discuss. Employees should be present during training, but they participate as they wish, voluntarily. The emphasis of the training is *not* to tell employees what they need to do and how to think, but to provide them with resources and other information so that they become motivated to develop their own emotional- and spiritual-survival practices, the ones that will work best for them.

After introducing the philosophy, the team can encourage a more inclusive buy-in by handing out an agency-wide survey. Responses will need to be anonymous. The purpose of the survey is to elicit input from all employees regarding how their jobs have adversely affected them, what they currently do for their own emotional/physical/mental/spiritual wellness, and what type of training they would like to see offered in order to address those issues. After one year, a follow-up survey can be conducted to monitor the effectiveness of the training and to solicit additional input. (See the sample "Wellness Program Survey" on page 233.)

BeSTOW Training Concepts

With input from the survey responses, the BeSTOW team can begin developing concepts of an agency wellness program to provide targeted wellness practices for emotional and spiritual survival. The following are examples of the training concepts developed at my agency over three years — concepts that would be effective for any first-responder agency or organization.

Wellness library. At our agency, we have a wellness library with books and DVDs that are checked out by officers and dispatchers.

These books and DVDs specifically address first-responder stress management, care and support, PTSD, suicide awareness and prevention, and emotional-spiritual survival issues, and they have proven to be a tremendous resource for employees. The library has also provided voluminous material for use in lineup training, scenario-based training, and periodic training bulletins.

For agencies in need of training funds, the Walmart Foundation offers community grants (typically around $1,200 but as high as $5,000). The application process is very simple. As my agency's wellness coordinator, I received several such grants over the years to help supply our wellness library and other wellness resources. To apply, see https://walmart.org/how-we-give/local-community -grants.

Lineup training. Members of the BeSTOW team provide periodic lineup training on the theme of emotional survival for all squads and units.

Training bulletins. We have developed dozens of such bulletins for all employees, providing training and resources on suicide awareness and prevention, preparing for and preventing PTSD, managing hypervigilance, stress management, ways to support an officer after a critical incident, support groups for spouses of law-enforcement officers, ways your family can support you, emotional-survival techniques, ways to maintain a healthy diet and get good sleep, the nobility of public service, and many other topics.

Field training. The BeSTOW philosophy has been incorporated into the field-training manual, where new employees are informed about the wellness program and the critical need to develop their own emotional- and spiritual-survival wellness practices to sustain them throughout their careers.

Mentors. BeSTOW team members volunteer to become mentors for academy recruits, to support them throughout the academy process.

Academy graduation. Upon graduation from the academy, the agency holds a dinner for the graduates and their families. At the celebration, training is provided regarding emotional survival. Also, spouses of longtime officers discuss with the families how to support their officer spouse or parent, and what they can expect from a law-enforcement profession. During this event, copies of this book as well as *Emotional Survival for Law Enforcement* by Kevin Gilmartin and *I Love a Cop* by Ellen Kirschman are given to the families.

Debriefing individuals involved in past critical incidents. The BeSTOW/peer-support team has debriefed individuals involved in past critical incidents, including officer-involved shootings, not for tactical purposes but for emotional- and spiritual-survival lessons and peer-support training. From this process we have learned more effective ways to support and care for officers and dispatchers immediately after a critical incident and beyond. Those involved in the critical incidents discuss how they felt the agency treated them, what made them feel supported, what upset them or made them feel resentful toward the agency, what people did or said that helped or hurt, and what could have been done that would have been more effective.

Support from home. We provide information about local support groups for law-enforcement wives/spouses, encouraging life partners to become involved. It is imperative to interest the spouses of emergency first responders in becoming active partners in their loved ones' emotional survival, so that they can most effectively support their public-servant family members. Positive home support is critical for the emotional and spiritual wellness of any first responder. (See chapter 10 for more information.)

Spouse debriefings. With the assistance of a department psychologist, the BeSTOW/peer-support team holds debriefings for the spouses of employees involved in critical incidents. A separate critical-incident debriefing is conducted with just the employees directly involved, along with peer-support team members, a chaplain, and the agency psychologist.

In-service training. BeSTOW training is included in periodic in-service and advanced officer-training courses that focus on stress management, suicide awareness and prevention, nutrition and health, and emotional-spiritual survival.

Involvement in the community. In order to connect with the community in a positive, constructive way that counteracts the negative aspect of police work, the BeSTOW team developed a very successful four-day Police Youth Leadership Camp, hosted by the department and facilitated by employees, to teach twenty-five high school students each summer about leadership skills, community volunteer service, and ethics. (For more information, see my article "Police Youth Leadership Camp: Influencing Young Lives" in the *FBI Law Enforcement Bulletin*: https://leb.fbi .gov/articles/featured-articles/police-youth-leadership-camp -influencing-young-lives.)

For the past twenty-five years, our agency has also identified four or five poor families from our schools each Christmas. We collect money from agency employees, buy several gifts for the children, invite the families to the police department for a Christmas dinner just before Christmas, and provide needed help to the families.

We also have formed a foundation called Officers Helping East County Youth. After identifying children who want to play sports but lack funds or equipment, we use our collected monies and sporting equipment donated from local businesses to sponsor them.

Community outreach is essential for an agency wellness program. It not only connects the first responders with the community and helps them to heal from past traumas, but it enhances the image of the agency, increases community support and involvement, and allows for greater positive interaction with the community served. Whenever you make a difference in the community, you are making a difference toward your own health, wellness, and survivability.

Bulletin board. Maintain a department wellness information board.

Interfaith Council collaboration. Members of the BeSTOW team have given presentations to the local Interfaith Council, and our wellness coordinator now attends their meetings. The Interfaith Council of La Mesa is a group of forty-four faith organizations. By explaining the BeSTOW philosophy to them, we have gained their assistance and support for our employees as needs arise; and we offer our assistance by partnering with the faith organizations in their community-supporting efforts. We have had professional members of these organizations volunteer to offer training and information about finances, fitness, stress management, nutrition, and other subjects.

PTSD pamphlet and information fliers. We distribute a twenty-seven-page pamphlet titled *PTSD: Not All Wounds Are Visible*, which describes PTSD, its symptoms, coping strategies, and ways to mitigate adverse effects on children in the home. Additionally, we provide BeSTOW information fliers to new employees and distribute them in the agency.

Quarterly agency wellness newsletter. We produce the newsletter *Vitality through Emotional Survival Training*, also known as *The VEST*, which supplies descriptions of physical challenges that encourage officers to maintain fitness and to compete with other employees, nutrition and diet information, Q&As and other information from the agency psychologist, details about group recreational activities and excursions, news about agency sports teams, schedules for upcoming trainings, and emotional-spiritual survival information.

Wellness retreat. This two-day health and wellness retreat at a local nature preserve includes workshops on PTSD, first-responder relationships, stress and coping strategies, and emotional survival.

Wellness assessments in yearly evaluations. Consider including in employees' annual evaluations a section where the supervisor discusses wellness with the employees. The supervisor would ask what they or the agency can do to support and help the employees, as well as discuss agency resources for wellness and encourage the employees to develop their own personal wellness programs.

Fifteen-day challenge. Self-improvement is an essential wellness concept. I've developed a fifteen-day challenge to encourage first responders to focus on wellness concepts that can be practiced throughout the day. This challenge has served to enhance the quality of my personal and professional life. The fifteen-day challenge is described in detail at the end of this chapter.

Other BeSTOW Efforts

Other agencies using the BeSTOW philosophy have continued to develop new efforts. Consider adopting any of the following ideas:

- Produce a brochure for family members that discusses emotional- and spiritual-survival issues; ways to support first responders; spousal-support-group information; and chaplain, peer-support, and counseling services offered by the agency, along with contact information.
- Encourage voluntary annual check-ins with a peer-support team member at the time of annual evaluations. This provides an opportunity for employees to talk about any issues they desire to discuss and to receive

updated emotional- and spiritual-survival and wellness information.

- Develop officer-death and serious-injury protocols pertaining to a peer-support response to assist the injured employee and the family.
- Adopt a policy of giving employees ten hours of time off in exchange for seeing a qualified therapist trained in trauma for an annual emotional-survival and wellness checkup. This would be completely voluntary and confidential, but encouraged by the first-responder agency.
- Develop a one- or two-day Family Academy, in which family members are introduced to the functions and culture of your agency and ways to support their first-responder spouse or parent. They can also be informed about services and resources available.
- Have the agency psychologist teach all staff members the signs of PTSD, ways to approach officers who may be suffering symptoms, and how to talk to officers about getting help or referrals when needed.
- Have the police psychologist teach employees how to prepare for and mitigate the effects of acute stress and PTSD that they may develop.
- Have a registered dietitian provide training on proper nutrition, energy drinks and other caffeinated beverages, and overall health and wellness issues.
- Have a financial planner provide training on financial wellness and sound financial practices.
- Develop some type of emotional-survival closed-network connection through social media, possibly through Facebook or Twitter or both. This would provide an easy way to disseminate information about available training and resources.

- Have retired employees and a retirement planner supply information on how to plan and prepare for retirement.
- Coordinate a countywide, three-day emotional-survival/wellness conference for emergency first responders.
- Develop a website on wellness that can only be accessed by first responders in the county. The site can include information about resources and training contributed by other agencies, best practices, peer-support and wellness teams, agency instructions and general orders related to peer-support teams and functions, wellness newsletters, and other wellness information.
- Have the agency's health insurance providers come to the agency to provide free health appraisals, training, and information.

A wellness program incorporating the BeSTOW philosophy can be anything that addresses the ongoing emotional- and spiritual-survival needs and well-being of any particular first-responder agency. The essential component is the support of top management and the employee union, as well as buy-in from various units throughout the agency on the line level. Most of the concepts developed in the program should come from the line-level employees, based on their particular needs. The BeSTOW team should meet regularly to develop new ideas and to sustain the program. Developing the BeSTOW philosophy into proactive training and effective resources is a long-term process and must be a continuous effort in order to be most effective.

In April 2012, San Diego County became the first known county in the nation where all law-enforcement agencies agreed to form a wellness committee with a representative of every first-responder agency in the county, including police, fire, emergency medical services, prison corrections, probation and parole agencies, police psychologists, and military police. The committee members have been working to learn from each other and to develop emotional- and spiritual-survival wellness practices for the five thousand peace officers in the county. The initial objective of this one-of-a-kind committee was to develop a peer-support team and foundation for all agencies within the county, as well as a website used for emotional-survival resources and training.

On the night of August 19, 2011, the La Mesa Police Department's BeSTOW philosophy would be challenged. After one year, would the effects of the BeSTOW training make a difference in the careers and lives of six officers who were about to face the ultimate critical incident? Or, as in years past, would these officers suffer irreversible emotional trauma? Chapter 12 describes how the wellness program and the BeSTOW philosophy saved the career and most probably the life of one of the officers.

Giving Back to the Community as Part of the BeSTOW Philosophy: Making a Difference

Discovering ways to give back to the community you serve is an integral component of an active BeSTOW philosophy. Remaining engaged with the community renews your spirit and desire to serve. Below are several wellness initiatives that employees at my agency have undertaken that have enhanced their well-being and the well-being of those they helped.

One officer developed a charitable organization that raised approximately $5,000 and distributed it to poor student athletes to enable them to participate in sports.

Currently, 20 percent of agency personnel are participating in a physical-wellness challenge, with fellow employees assisting as mentors and coaches. Fifteen employees are actively involved with peer support and developing the BeSTOW philosophy, providing essential around-the-clock support to employees.

At the time of this writing, 12 percent of the agency is training for a half marathon in Las Vegas. Several have already participated in half or full marathons after being trained by a lieutenant on her own time. Nearly 20 percent of the individuals in this agency have participated as runners or support persons in the annual Baker to Vegas Challenge, a 120-mile desert relay run from Baker, California, to Las Vegas.

The La Mesa Police Officers Association is actively involved in supporting local charities and educational scholarships. Officers coordinated a charity golf tournament and raised $9,600 for the local animal shelter. Each Christmas, several officers participate in the local Shop with a Cop program, in which officers partner with poor children and shop with them at a local Target store, using donated funds. The children each get to spend $100 on themselves and their family.

Over the past twenty-five years, employees have donated over $15,000 to buy food and toys for more than sixty poor families as part of our annual Christmas Family Adoption program. Our agency has donated food to a local food bank for Thanksgiving for the past twenty-three years. Several officers over the years have, on their own, provided clothing, food, and assistance to local homeless people. Several employees volunteer their time to facilitate the annual Police Department Youth Leadership Camp, while many others volunteer as local coaches.

The police department recently adopted a local middle school, where 53 percent of the students (more than three hundred students) live under the poverty line. Thousands of dollars were raised to provide library books, computers, sports team memberships, memberships in youth facilities, before- and after-school programs, a life-skills class, a running club in which officers run with the kids after school, and a police boot camp.

After seeing a malnourished little girl living in the filthiest, most deplorable conditions, one officer convinced the transient, drug-addicted mother to allow him and his wife to adopt the girl. The officer raised the girl as his own. This was an unbelievable act of compassion that truly exemplified the essence of a first responder.

This is just a very small sampling of some of the efforts undertaken to promote wellness of mind, body, and spirit. Promoting the positive, in order to counterbalance all the negative we experience, enables us to maintain health and vitality in service and to process many of the traumas we have experienced.

Self-Improvement as an Integral Part of the BeSTOW Philosophy: The Fifteen-Day Challenge Wellness Initiative

Self-improvement is a vital wellness concept. I have developed the following fifteen-day challenge to focus attention on specific objectives that I know from personal experience can enhance the quality of first responders' personal and professional lives. By giving a full day's attention to a specific goal that can be practiced throughout the day, you can develop positive qualities that, over time, may become a natural part of your character.

Over the years this fifteen-day challenge has enabled me to maintain and enhance the wellness of my spirit. It has served to keep me grounded and helped me to maintain a positive perspective on life and work. As with everything in life, you get out of this challenge only what you are willing to put in. Commit to this fifteen-day challenge, one day at a time, with all your heart and motivation. In order to change, heal, and create positive circumstances, we must first be changed within. Periodically return to this challenge and repeat it for the most effective results. At least once a year, on your anniversary hire date, is a good time to repeat this practice.

Day 1. Self-Awareness

Write down in detail why you became a first responder: What is your purpose in doing this work? How has the job adversely affected you, your outlook on life, and your primary relationships? What value do you get, and should you get, from this work?

Challenge: Rededicate yourself to the purpose of protecting and giving life to others. Write down what your family, spouse, friends, work colleagues, and community need from you, and focus on that rather than what you want from them. Do not focus on what you think you deserve; rather, focus on what you can give. Make a list of all of the positive values of public service.

Day 2. Goals

Redefine your goals. Having short-term, intermediate, and long-term goals is essential to remaining motivated and grounded.

Challenge: Write down at least one realistic short-term goal, an intermediate goal, and a long-term goal. Describe what you can do each day toward achieving each goal — even something as simple as reminding yourself about them each morning. As goals are achieved, replace them with new ones.

Day 3. Communication

Practicing effective communication while sharing your experiences, thoughts, and emotions is essential to sustain not only a healthy spirit but also healthy relationships.

Challenge: Actively work each day at developing a genuine interest in others, especially the most important people in your life — even the difficult people. Learn to ask questions of other people to connect with them, to find out more about them, and simply to get them to talk about themselves. And listen to them more than you talk. Develop a strong foundation in your relationships with others, and support them, by engaging and talking with them — even when you don't feel like it.

Day 4. Relationships

As Helen Keller said, the most important things in life cannot be seen or touched but are felt with the heart. Write down whom your most important relationships are with and what makes them so important.

Challenge: Tell or write someone today about how much you appreciate them and what they mean to you. Write down what you can do to consistently work at improving these relationships. Specify what *you* can do, independently of how the other person may respond.

Day 5. Expressing Love

The greatest motivators, inspirations, purposes, and sources of contentment in life come from living expressions of love. This is evidenced by the fact that when people are near death, they inevitably think of their loved ones and the love they experienced throughout their lives. They do not think about what they achieved, or what positions they may have held, or how much money they were able to accumulate. They do not wish they had spent more of their lives at work. The biggest regret of most people is that they did not spend enough time with their kids. They wish they had been better husbands or wives, sons or daughters, fathers or mothers. At the end of life, people inevitably reach out to their loved ones and want only to be with them one last time.

Challenge: Show your most important people that they are the most important things in your life by what you do each day. Show them — beyond words, through the quality and quantity of time you spend with them — how valued they are to you. Do something special with them this day.

Day 6. Forgiveness

Not forgiving yourself and others causes more discontent and anxiety than nearly anything else.

Challenge: The original meaning of the word *forgiveness* is "to let go." Choosing not to forgive someone — harboring ill will toward someone, no matter how seemingly justified — hurts only you, not the other person. Ask someone you have wronged in the past to forgive you. And forgive someone you believe has wronged you.

Day 7. Letting Go

We naturally tend to identify with negative emotions and harbor negative feelings. Negative thoughts and negative emotions only poison your spirit and prevent you from enjoying the highest quality of life.

Challenge: Make a conscious effort to become aware of every negative thought or negative emotion this day. Then, consciously let go of that negativity and replace it with a positive thought, a positive affirmation, or a remembrance of a positive feeling. Try this day to live only in the present moment, to be completely mindful and present within the moment at hand.

Day 8. Compassion

The most satisfying and meaningful life is built on selfless motivation, self-giving behavior, and compassion toward others. The quality of our lives and the well-being of our spirits increase the more we recognize that life is not all about us. The more your life is about others and their well-being, the more you will find peace and contentment.

Challenge: Do something kind and unexpected today for someone else. Make a habit of looking for unexpected things to do for others.

Day 9. Self-Improvement

Maintaining a vibrant, healthy spirit depends on progress and the development of a finer character. People improve their character only through consistent effort. Write down words that describe what kind of person you are, what kind of person you are becoming, and what kind of person you would like to be. List the ideal characteristics you would like to attain.

Challenge: Identify one negative or bad habit you wish you did not have. Replace that habit with a positive, good one. Each day, work at developing those ideal characteristics you hope to attain. Practice developing the habit of positive thinking.

Day 10. Exercise

Few things will enhance the wellness of your spirit more than consistent exercise.

Challenge: If you are not consistently exercising (three to four days a week), develop a reasonable exercise plan that you can maintain. Start it today. If you are already exercising, evaluate how effective and consistent it has been and resolve to increase your effort.

Day 11. Gratitude

It is nearly impossible for your spirit to be depressed while you are feeling thankful. The consistent practice of being thankful for all the good in your life will help sustain your spirit and keep you from sinking into depression.

Challenge: Write a detailed list of everything you are grateful for, no matter how small; list everything good in your life now or in the past. After one week, create a new list and see how many more things you have realized you actually have to be grateful about.

Day 12. Silence

In silence we can come to know ourselves and our needs. Without the constant distractions of life, we tend to unleash creative ideas. Silence is a way to get in touch with yourself and to become centered on what you value in life. Silence gives you a new perspective on issues and problems.

Challenge: Use this day as a day of silence. Try not to speak unless you absolutely have to. Don't listen to the radio in the car. Don't use an iPod, television, computer game, or anything else with sound. If you are in the habit of falling asleep with the television on, go to bed without it. Use this day of silence to think more clearly, to feel, and to be present.

Day 13. Speaking Kindly and Positively

We often use speech to broadcast and reinforce negative thinking and negative emotions. Your speech may promote your own ego and self-interest, and you may use it against others. This can have a highly damaging effect on your spirit.

Challenge: Use this day to speak only positively and helpfully. Do not speak negatively about anyone, about your agency, or about yourself.

Day 14. Making the Right Choices

The dozens of choices you make every day determine and sustain the quality of your professional and personal lives. The constructive use of choice and free will can immediately begin to enhance the wellness of your spirit and the quality of your life. Just becoming aware that you have choices to make, instead of living on autopilot, is the first step. Strive to have every choice you make be the one that is most compassionate, life affirming, and productive of wellness.

Challenge: Make a list of three choices you regret. Make a list of the reasons why you made those choices. What was the motivation behind them? Write down what you will do to more consistently make constructive choices that are compassionate and life affirming. Examine the motivation behind why you do anything.

And/or just for today, make three good choices. Eat X for lunch instead of Y, say no to drinks with your friend, turn off the TV, and so on.

Day 15. Righting Past Wrongs

Your spirit may be heavily weighed down by things you have said and done in the past and still regret.

Challenge: Make a list of every person you have wronged in one way or another, in both your personal and professional lives. Each day, do something to rectify one of those wrongs. Then the next day, rectify the wrong you committed against the next person on your list, until the list is exhausted.

Self-Awareness Questions to Help Define Your Purpose

What provides you with a sense of purpose and meaning in life, and how can that be nurtured?

As first responders, we tend to lose touch with those positive, nurturing things that used to provide purpose in our lives. This question will help you reconnect with what is truly important in your life —

what is life sustaining, what sustains your spirit. It may also help you realize that you have been neglecting those positive things and what you can do to reconnect with them.

What do the community, the agency, your colleagues, and your family need from you?

A natural tendency for first responders is to eventually succumb to the "victim mentality," in which you see yourself as being victimized by society, the agency, colleagues, the "system," and so on. By learning to turn your focus away from yourself and to center on what others need from you, not what you want from them, you will help prevent the onset of the victim mentality.

Chapter Nine

PEER SUPPORT

Hard times don't create heroes.
It is during the hard times when the "hero"
within us is revealed.

— BOB RILEY

Ron served as one of eight volunteers on his agency's peer-support team at the fire department. He was always ready to assist when his fellow firefighters or paramedics approached him for advice, help, and assistance with work issues or personal problems. He did the greatest amount of good for his team, however, by keeping his eyes open and reaching out, trying to help his colleagues before they came to him.

Over a period of several weeks, Ron noticed that Jason, a firefighter colleague, didn't seem to be quite his normal self. The usually friendly Jason was isolating himself and remaining very quiet. One morning after breakfast, Ron approached him and said, "How are you? You haven't seemed yourself lately. Is everything all right?" Jason answered with a short "I'm fine." Ron told him, "Okay, Jason, but I want you to know that I am here for you if there's anything you want to talk about." He gave him a pat on the arm and started to walk away, when Jason called him back, saying that actually there was something that had been bothering him.

Jason said his divorce would be final in another two weeks. He was having problems focusing at work and felt like he didn't care about anything anymore. Ron asked Jason if he needed anything immediately, and Jason promised him that he would be fine. Ron assured him he was always there if he wanted to talk, and he also gave Jason contact information for the fire department's counselor in case he ever needed it.

Over the next two weeks Ron checked in frequently with Jason, offered help, and called him from time to time on days off. He spent some time with Jason off duty, helping him put up a fence at his house and just hanging out. One night Ron got a call at 2 AM from Jason, who sounded very depressed and said he needed to talk. Ron immediately got out of bed and met Jason at an all-night breakfast joint. There, he listened as Jason poured out his heart about his divorce and other personal problems.

Over the next week Ron noticed that Jason was starting to look and act more like his normal self. One day Jason came up to him and said, "Hey, I never really thanked you for looking out for me and meeting me that night. I would never tell anyone else this, but as I called you that night I was holding a gun in my other hand. I was ready to end it all, but when you agreed to see me, I thought I could just wait and see. I feel much better now — but I know I wouldn't be here if you hadn't shown up that night. Thanks."

A dedicated peer-support team member can have a dramatic impact on an employee's morale. Peer-support team members are trusted, experienced colleagues (current or retired) who offer confidential assistance and guidance in times of stress and crisis. These teams are so effective because emergency-first-responder peers uniquely understand the stress and emotional problems of the profession. An active and respected peer-support team is a vital part of an overall wellness program for first responders.

In the 1950s, police agencies in New York, Boston, and Chicago began developing components of a peer-support program to address alcoholism and related issues within their departments. In 1968, the Los Angeles Police Department developed the first in-house behavioral science unit, which, in 1981, resulted in the nation's first officially sanctioned, department-sponsored peer-support program. The International Association of Chiefs of Police currently endorses peer-support programs and provides general guidelines and operational standards for such programs. They have also endorsed critical-incident stress management training and debriefings, typically in conjunction with a mental health counselor. (See www.theiacp.org for more details.)

Over the decades, all the emergency-first-responder professions have clearly grown aware of the critical need to have a program of confidential and trusted support and assistance for their members, by their members. Given the fact that these emotionally, mentally, and spiritually challenging professions are closed and insulated, and that members have learned not to trust anyone "outside" their profession, first responders are uniquely receptive to assistance offered from an experienced and trusted peer, someone who understands their job, their frustrations, and their pain. Peer-support programs have consistently proven to be far more effective than reliance on individual officers to seek professional help on their own.

Peer supporters are *not* mental health counselors or therapists, but are trained, experienced, and trusted peers who provide an invaluable resource to colleagues by listening to them, supporting them, and assisting them in any way necessary. They help in countless ways by offering various forms of support and assistance to an employee (or to an employee's family members) who may be suffering from cancer or any other serious illness, emotional distress, acute stress, symptoms of PTSD, job-related stress and problems, and any marital or family issues that could potentially cause problems at work or a personal or professional crisis. Peer supporters also help with critical-incident stress management debriefings and defusings and provide pre-crisis preparation through education that enhances coping skills and stress management. Basically, peer supporters provide any needed assistance on a confidential, nonjudgmental, and caring basis.

Not everyone within an agency can be an effective peer-support team member. Those who are selected must be acceptable to all employees throughout the agency, including civilian employees. Far too often dispatchers and other civilian employees, who can suffer just as much as any first responder, are neglected. These employees need peer support as much as anyone else. Peer-support team members must be experienced, must have excellent interpersonal and listening skills, and must have earned the trust and confidence of their peers and superiors on the job. They must be approachable, and they should both have and project a positive, caring, and empathetic attitude. A team member who lacks these qualities can potentially have a devastating and demoralizing effect on the peer-support program. There should be a process for the careful selection of team members, as well as a process for eliminating anyone who does not work out.

It is an unfortunate fact that gossip, backbiting, rumors, and hazing within first-responder communities are commonplace — and extremely detrimental to morale. Peer supporters need to play a role in calling attention to and dismissing this sort of behavior, which will otherwise have a debilitating effect on the entire agency.

The most important job of an effective peer-support team member is to listen. A peer supporter asks questions and possibly talks about his or her own related experiences that may be helpful, as opposed to giving advice or telling someone what to do. They are always nonjudgmental, and their prime concern is always the well-being of their coworkers. A peer supporter will typically ask how a coworker is doing, whether they need anything, or what can be done to help. Often, just having a peer to talk with in a confidential setting can significantly help the employee process the problem more positively, because he or she is relating to a coworker who has likely experienced similar circumstances.

Peer-support teams can be created and maintained with little or no expense. Though it is recommended that team members go through some training regarding critical-incident stress management, trauma intervention, and problem solving, most of the training takes place on the job. That is, it will come from the varied experiences of team members themselves during monthly or periodic meetings. There are also professionals within each community who may be willing to donate time to provide stress-management and related training. Chaplains typically provide free training, too, on such matters as grieving, assisting and supporting others, and other topics. In fact, an integral component of a peer-support team should be a chaplain program. (Chaplain programs are discussed in chapter 11.)

Responsibilities of a Peer-Support Team

An effective peer-support team serves the agency in the following ways:

1. Convey trustworthiness and confidentiality to employees who seek assistance from the peer-support program or who may be referred by another concerned employee.

2. Attend peer-support training and periodic meetings to discuss issues and develop training. I would assign a peer-support member, on a rotating basis, to give the other team members training for ten to fifteen minutes on any subject of wellness they desired during the meetings.

3. Provide assistance and support to both civilian and sworn employees as needed.

4. Assist employees by referring them to the appropriate resource (professional or otherwise) when necessary, as the employee wishes.

5. Listen, offer support, and reach out to peers to connect with them and ensure they are doing all right; offer any assistance that may be requested.

6. Agree to be contacted, and if necessary, respond at any hour to assist an employee.

7. Coordinate employee and family events, picnics, and other activities to build a well-rounded family support system for the agency's employees.

8. Listen and talk with an employee after a critical incident or crisis, or during any time of emotional distress.

9. Provide information on resources available, such as the Employee Assistance Program, Alcoholics Anonymous or other substance abuse programs, credit and financial counseling, chaplain services, and other professional services.

10. Conduct or assist in critical-incident stress management defusings (for relatively immediate decompression after a less serious incident). This is a three-phase, structured,

small-group discussion provided within hours of a crisis for purposes of assessment, triaging, and acute-symptom mitigation. (See page 132.)

11. Conduct critical-incident stress management debriefings (for more serious critical incidents, such as a shooting), in conjunction with a qualified therapist acting as the facilitator. (See page 129.)

12. Provide proactive training, information, and other resources to employees throughout the agency to help them learn to become more effective at processing stress, trauma, and other adverse effects of the job.

13. Provide ongoing emotional-survival training, suicide awareness and prevention, and wellness training and information for the agency.

14. Make periodic visits to roll calls / lineup trainings. The more visible the peer supporters are, and the more they discuss how they can be useful, the more they will be utilized.

The peer-support team leader should identify appropriate ongoing training for peer-support members. Relevant introductory and continuing training for team members could cover the following topics:

- Confidentiality
- Role conflict
- Limits and liability
- Ethical issues
- Communication facilitation and listening skills
- Nonverbal communication
- Problem assessment
- Problem-solving skills
- Cross-cultural issues
- Psychological trauma and coping methods

- Stress management
- Burnout
- Grief management
- Domestic violence
- Suicide assessment
- Crisis management
- Trauma intervention
- Alcohol and substance abuse
- When to seek mental health consultation and referral information
- Critical-incident stress management and debriefings
- Emotional-survival training

How to Establish and Maintain a Peer-Support Team

Initially, anyone who wants to initiate a peer-support program must gain the support of the chief or agency head and management, since support from top management is essential for an effective and lasting peer-support program. There are volumes of research available that convey the need for and the multiple benefits of such a program for emergency first responders. That, coupled with the overwhelming evidence of the significant emotional and psychological trauma prevalent throughout first-responder professions, should make the need for such a beneficial program evident.

Those interested in establishing a peer-support program should initiate a steering committee to begin the process. The steering committee should be made up of dedicated and trusted peers who are passionate about the well-being of their colleagues. Money should not be an issue in establishing the program, since training can be solicited from professionals in the community, as well as from other team members. If professionals are not available and there are no funds for training, simply having a dedicated team of peers who are devoted to the wellness of their colleagues, and who meet regularly and learn from each other's experiences, is extremely beneficial to the organization.

The team should be governed by a written policy, department instructions, a manual, or other established rules and regulations that provide the operating guidelines for the peer-support program. Creating such guidelines is the primary function of the steering committee. This written policy should delineate the purpose, mission, and role of the peer-support team. It should further delineate the selection process, the desired qualities or amount of experience sought in prospective team members, the method and reasons for removing a team member, the training required for team members, the chain of command, confidentiality guidelines, and a list of incidents requiring a peer-support response. (Please see the end of this chapter for links to helpful resources.)

The chain of command for the peer-support team (the team leader and the wellness coordinator in charge of the peer-support team) works best if it is a direct link to the agency head in order to maintain confidentiality and to have an effective way for several sworn and nonsworn personnel from various commands to answer to the same command pertaining to peer-support issues. This keeps confidential information private from supervisors of employees who are experiencing personal or professional issues. The most effective way to organize the chain of command is to have all peer-support team members answer directly to a team leader, who in turn answers to a wellness-program coordinator. The coordinator answers directly to the agency head.

The selection of peer-support team members must be taken seriously. There should be a recommendation and testing process in order to ensure that the most interested, most trusted, and most experienced and effective people are selected.

Confidentiality is the cornerstone of an effective peer-support program. Department policy on confidentiality, as outlined in the written guidelines, must be strictly enforced. These rules and guidelines concerning confidentiality should follow the laws of your state. One breach of trust can destroy any peer-support program. However, there are legally sanctioned times when confidentiality must be broken: disclosures of child abuse, elder abuse, or domestic violence; criminal threats; or when suicide is threatened.

Depending upon case law and statute, under very limited circumstances a peer supporter can be ordered to disclose information pertaining to a serious internal affairs investigation. (However, a chaplain is prohibited by law from disclosing any such information in all circumstances.) A peer-support team member can avoid ever being in this situation by not discussing criminal behavior or policy violations with a coworker. In such circumstances, the peer supporter is there to provide whatever help or assistance may be useful, not to listen to criminal or agency violation disclosures.

Once a peer-support team has been established and written guidelines and policy have been approved by department management, the team must work to become accepted throughout the agency. Team members can help this process along by providing information about what the peer-support team is and how team members can be a resource to all employees.

Team members should meet regularly, usually monthly or quarterly, to debrief and discuss peer-support situations, conduct training, and discuss ways of providing resources and assistance to employees in need. Meetings need to be meaningful.

The value of a peer-support team cannot be overstated. Providing a means for employees to support, assist, and help each other is the best mechanism to ensure a healthy organization. A peer-support team is an essential pillar of support for the emotional and spiritual survival and wellness of emergency first responders.

La Mesa police officer Tim Purdy discusses the critical importance of the peer-support team that aided him after he was involved in a fatal shooting:

I know that having a peer-support team is not something that should just be considered or something that "maybe we should do." It should definitely be something that every first-responder agency has. In my opinion, it's not clear how an agency can function and keep its officers healthy without one. I can tell you from my personal experience that if it weren't for our peer-support team and the BeSTOW philosophy at La Mesa Police, then most likely — I can't say this with 100 percent certainty, but I can tell you that I am fairly sure — I would not be here. I probably would not be married, and I would definitely not be a police officer anymore. Officer wellness is something that I am passionate about now, and I can't say enough about the critical importance of having a peer-support team.

The period after my shooting was very difficult for me and my family. I had to take a six-week leave of absence. At times I felt guilty about not coming back to work, and I had problems just dealing with everyday life. The peer-support team was there for me through it all. When you have that kind of support, which you don't even have to ask for — it's just automatically there for you — it's almost like an angel in disguise. I can't stress that enough. For me, the best thing was being able to talk about the incident, having people who understood and actually cared — not only my family but also everyone here at the police department, from the top down. They basically saved my life and saved my career.

Fire captain Dave Hardenburger discusses the crucial importance a peer-support critical-incident debriefing can have:

> Occasionally we'll have members of the community come straight to the fire station for help instead of calling 911. Usually it's because they are on their way to the hospital and the situation suddenly gets worse. Needless to say, when someone rings the doorbell for "walk-in" medical aid, it's usually serious.
>
> As my colleagues and I were enjoying a relatively slow morning on a very warm San Diego day, we were surprised by one of these walk-ins. As it turned out, this was the worst we had ever experienced. A hysterical young mother had brought two toddlers to the fire station because of a possible drowning. She was kicking the firehouse door as she screamed, holding both her lifeless babies, one under each arm.
>
> Performing CPR on one child is disturbing enough, but at this moment we were faced with trying to restore life to two toddlers: a brother and sister, both still in diapers. For those who don't know, doing CPR on a person is intense and emotional; it's a thousand times worse when you're dealing with children. And another thousand times more intense when you have kids at home around the same age.
>
> When paramedics arrived they could hear the screams of the frantic mother over the sound of their rig's engine. Rescuers frantically did everything they could with both of the lifeless kids, assisting with airway management, CPR, medication delivery — everything in a desperate and ultimately futile attempt to bring them back to life.
>
> In the background, during the frantic commotion, were two unmistakable and incredibly hard-to-shake sounds — the screams of a desperate mom slowly realizing her two babies were dead and the frantic voice of our most experienced

captain. *Both sent chills down my neck, because I could only imagine the feelings of the mother, and I recognized the near panic of an extremely experienced supervisor. For some reason, the mixture of those blood-curdling sounds continued to echo in my ears long after the lifeless toddlers were taken to the hospital, where they were pronounced dead.*

It's hard to explain why certain things stick in your mind, or why they can affect you so dramatically. When it happens, there's no mistaking it. The shrill screams of that mother's helpless voice will haunt me for a while, as will the unforgettable sight of those sweet, innocent babies — limp, cold, and lifeless — while the best-trained rescuers hopelessly worked on them. But even more disturbing for me was the fact that one of our bravest, most experienced, and most respected captains was so shaken that day. I witnessed a terrible event that showed that the very best among us is vulnerable. I kept wondering, how vulnerable was I? And the rest of my colleagues?

We are all desperately vulnerable to being shaken and to suffering emotionally from just doing our jobs. Our jobs deal with life and death, often affecting our own emotional well-being. It made me remember that we, as first responders, are all just human beings with emotions, worries, and fears who have an unquenchable desire to save everyone... and that sometimes we fail. When we fail, someone else doesn't get to see their baby, their mother, their spouse, ever again.

Later that day, the peer-support team held a defusing for all the medics, dispatchers, and fire personnel involved. It was a tremendously beneficial thing to do, because it gave us all a chance to hear from each other and to start to process the terrible event we had just experienced. A lot of people, including myself, would have struggled much more had the peer-support team not been there to help us through it.

Since many of the rescuers continued to show obvious signs of being bothered, one week later the peer-support team conducted a more detailed debriefing of the incident. I cannot stress enough how beneficial that was for everyone. It was a crucial link that enabled us to more effectively process what happened and how we were affected, and to move forward.

Self-Awareness Questions to Define Your Motivation

What is your motivation for your life and why you work? What is your motivation for being married or otherwise joining with a life partner, for being a parent, or for doing anything? Are you motivated primarily by your heart? Is your motivation selfless? Is your motivation conducive to a peaceful, happy, and contented life?

Our reasons for doing anything reflect our hearts, our wellness, and our sense of purpose. By examining what truly motivates us, we can work to improve how we spend our time, how we conduct our relationships, and our effect on others. Offering yourself for service as a peer-support person or in any other capacity in order to be of positive use to others is one of the best things you can do to nurture your spirit.

You can find several sample peer-support program policies on the California Peer Support Association website at www.california peersupport.org. The International Association of Chiefs of Police and *Police Chief Magazine* offer additional peer-support guidelines and information at www.policechiefmagazine.org (enter "peer support guidelines" in the website search box).

Chapter Ten

SUPPORT FROM HOME

In everyone's life, at some time, our inner fire goes out.
It is then burst into flame by an encounter
with another human being. We should all be thankful
for those people who rekindle the inner spirit.

— ALBERT SCHWEITZER

Greg, a firefighter, had just finished up a three-day shift, returning from his second dead-baby call in less than twenty-four hours. Today's call involved the suffocation of an eight-month-old baby girl. The previous call involved the death of a five-month-old boy as a result of sudden infant death syndrome.

Over his eight-year career, Greg had grown accustomed to death and tragedy, so much so that he was numb, rarely feeling much anymore, either at work or at home. Every medical-assistance run caused him to become more disconnected and distant, no longer the man that his wife had once been so proud of. Now she didn't even recognize this shell of the man she had once known. Just about the only feeling Greg had anymore was the foreboding he felt when driving home each night.

Alicia, Greg's wife of nine years, had given up. She was tired of being married to a man who was physically present but who wore a blank stare as if he were a million miles away. She didn't understand how Greg could use his favorite chair as a pacifier, why he never wanted to make any decisions, and why he never wanted to go anywhere or do anything fun anymore. She thought she had tried everything, including trying to get him to talk, nagging him, yelling at him, not talking to him, getting angry at him, being more sexual, withholding sex, and pleading with him. The more she pushed, the more he pulled away.

Alicia was frustrated at what their once-good marriage had become. She felt frightened, lonely, and helpless. Meanwhile, coming home, Greg drove more slowly than usual, relishing the last few minutes of peace he had before walking inside the house and being immediately barraged with questions, demands, and angry remarks, facing a now-unsympathetic life partner. Neither one of them had ever realized that the insidious nature of a first responder's career could easily change a loved one into someone you no longer recognized.

Inside, Greg felt just as helpless as Alicia. He didn't know how he had become so calloused and distant, or just how bad the state of his marriage had become. On this night, Alicia sat resolutely at the kitchen table, waiting for him to come home so she could tell him she wanted a divorce....

The most-often overlooked pillar of support for emergency first responders is the most essential — support from home. Without understanding and care from partners and family, emotional-survival support at work is ineffectual. Unfortunately, life partners of emergency first responders receive no training at all regarding how to care for a spouse who has devoted his or her life to serving others. That needs to change. Any agency wellness program needs to find ways to include family, to provide them with resources and training and incorporate them as emotional-survival partners.

All intimate relationships have their difficulties; living with an emergency first responder is particularly difficult and offers a unique set of challenges. However, when life partners become aware of the special needs of their first responders — how they can most effectively address the emotional and spiritual wellness of their first responders — life at home can be far more peaceful and fulfilling. By learning how to nurture their first-responder spouses, they can become hidden partners in achieving overall wellness and emotional survival. Unfortunately, most first responders do just the opposite: they try not to involve their partners in their work. They want to shield the ones they love from the uglier side of the job.

It's important for you as a first responder to realize how invaluable support and understanding from home is to your wellness and emotional survival. Spouses do not need to know every last detail of the traumas their mates experience, but they must be allowed to care for and support them in their own way. Most spouses really don't want to hear the worst, but they definitely want to know that their mates are all right. Instead of building an emotional wall or pushing spouses away, first responders need to learn how to emotionally embrace their partners in life and make them the most important aspect of their lives. It's vital for you to tell your life partner what you need from them in terms of support and help. It's just as vital for you to ask them what they need from you, so both of you can purposefully support and care for each other in the ways the other needs.

Among the best books on supporting a life partner in an emergency-first-responder profession are *I Love a Cop: What Police Families Need to Know* or *I Love a Fire Fighter*, both by Ellen

Kirschman. These books discuss the benefits and emotional dangers of police or firefighter work, which correspond to those of any other first-responder profession. They describe how to manage the effects of trauma and acute stress, as well as the pressures of unpredictable schedules, long hours, and loneliness. Kirschman also provides an overview of the emotional, physical, and behavioral warning signs that can lead to PTSD, alcoholism, suicide, depression, and other emotional problems that spouses can be on the watch for.

As we discussed in chapter 3, female emergency first responders are particularly vulnerable to emotional and physical problems because a wife and mother is rarely ever allowed time alone to decompress from the hypervigilance roller coaster. Spouses of female emergency first responders need to realize the critical importance of allowing their life partners time to unwind after coming home. Without an opportunity to relax in the way that she chooses, even for a short period, the physiological and emotional turmoil that a female emergency first responder experiences can be dramatically heightened.

Spouse Support Groups

One of the most beneficial resources for spouses of first responders are spouse support groups. There are several such spouse support groups and resources, including the following:

- Thin Blue Line Foundation, https://thinbluelinefoundation .org/spouses
- The international Association of Chiefs of Police, www .theiacp.org/ICPRlawenforcementfamily (this site has lots of information, such as guidelines for organizing a spouse support group)

- Fire Engineering, www.fireengineering.com/articles/print
  /volume-162/issue-12/departments/fire-commentary/what
  -every-firefighter.html
- Firefighters' wives support group, http://cl-tina.starting
  again-ivil.tripod.com/support.html
- Operation Homefront, a military-home support group,
  www.operationhomefront.net
- Military Wives, a military-spouse support network, www
  .militarywives.com
- MilitarySOS, a support network for significant others,
  www.militarysos.com

Insights from First-Responder Spouses

I interviewed several long-term spouses of first responders and
asked them how a life partner can best support and care for their
first-responder mate. Their insightful advice is extremely useful
and just as applicable to the life partners of people in any other
first-responder profession, male or female. I've incorporated their
multiple replies into the following sections.

How Can You Best Support a First-Responder Mate, and What Might Be Inadvertently Harmful?

*"Create a stress-free home. Be positive, keep your spouse centered, and
enjoy each other. Be understanding. Listen to his needs, without forgetting your own."*

*"It's crucial that you learn to read your first-responder spouse and know
when he needs to talk and when he just needs time to be alone and process what he's feeling. Understand that sometimes distance is necessary
and that this need is not personal. When our mates are quiet or a little
distant, it isn't always about us. Most of the time they are trying to come*

to terms with issues on their own before they bring them to us. Giving them the time they need without feeling resentful is difficult but necessary. Recognize when your partner needs to talk, and make sure you are there for him when that time comes. It is valuable to learn to put your first-responder spouse's needs before your own at times."

"Complaining or trying to force your spouse to talk will ruin your marriage. Our spouses have chosen a life of service, and we need to step up, to be strong, independent partners who can lead our families. Complaining about the way things are will not change them; it will only make things worse."

"Remember that spending time with your spouse is precious; value it and make the most of it. Do not spend your precious time together complaining that he is never home and that you always have to do things alone. He knows that, and it hurts him as well. First responders see many terrible things in the course of doing their work. They want and need to be able to come home to a safe, peaceful, and loving home. If they know that at the end of their shift they will be greeted with complaints and arguments, they will likely choose to go elsewhere."

What Can the Spouse of a First Responder Expect, and How Will a First Responder Likely Change?

"Keep the lines of communication open without prying or nagging. Try to be patient. Your mate needs some downtime when he comes home so he can recharge, release the day, and tune in to being at home as a father and husband. However, continued isolation and disengagement from the family is not healthy. Ask your partner what they need from you and what strategies might be helpful to keep them active and engaged with life."

"Let your spouse know that you are always there for him whenever he needs you or wants to talk. Be there as a positive, understanding, nonjudgmental, and loving spouse who helps keep him well. You are an essential silent partner who aids in his emotional survival and ability to

process what he experiences at work. Remember that your spouse needs to be focused at work; his life and the safety of others depend on that. Don't get into arguments on the phone or discuss home issues because you need to talk about them. Your partner needs to remain focused at work to be safe."

"The life of a police wife is a constant roller coaster of emotion. Between shift work, overtime, court cases, the stress, and the critical incidents, life always seems to be changing. There is a lot more to being a police wife than spending nights and holidays alone. Remember that your mate would much rather be at home with you; the separation hurts both of you."

"Go on a ride-along to get a better understanding of what your spouse faces each day. You'll find that the second he puts on his uniform, he becomes more alert and more serious, begins multitasking, and becomes an energized decision maker. After ten to twelve hours of this, he may come home tired, remote, and grumpy, wanting to be left alone and not make any decisions. If your police spouse is doing something unacceptable to you, let him know what it is and how he may be changing. He may not be aware of it. Allow him to have some downtime when he comes home; he needs it."

After a Critical Incident, How Can You Best Support Your First-Responder Spouse?

"Right after an incident, you support him by focusing on him. Critical incidents are traumatic for both spouses, but being able to suppress your fears in front of him and lend support will help your mate get through the experience and know he can depend on you. When wives panic during these incidents, husbands tend to keep things from them, which creates distance in the relationship."

"Many officers want to protect and shelter their spouses from incidents in order to prevent any unnecessary worry. However, this builds barriers, and marriages slowly break apart as a result. Be the strong person that your spouse can depend on. Be the one he knows can handle anything. At

work, he has to be able to handle anything; at home you can provide him with a place where he knows someone else will take care of him without judging him, condemning him, or pressuring him to change."

"Long-term support means remembering the incident and its impact on him. Over time the papers will no longer publish stories about the incident; the lawsuit, if there is one, will subside; and coworkers will forget the incident ever happened. But your spouse will think about it every day, every time he puts on his uniform. That critical incident becomes a part of who he is, and he will forever be changed in some way by that incident."

"Never imply he should have already put something behind him. Some traumas may never go away; often, officers don't know how to place a traumatic event into proper perspective. That's why it is so important for the spouse to be patient, compassionate, empathetic, and understanding."

"Understand that the traumas of their career can cause an injury to their brain's ability to function normally and to process life. Research and learn about post-traumatic stress disorder [see www.ptsd.va.gov or www.emdria.org]. EMDR or other treatment therapies can heal PTSD."

Should You Tell Your Mate That He or She Is Changing, and If So, How Do You Get a Cooperative Response?

"Yes, communication is important. If a spouse is changing, it is a life partner's responsibility to bring it to his attention. There may be something going on that your mate has not mentioned. Be sensitive to the situation. Be honest and choose a good time and place. Make sure that you are not accusing or complaining but being supportive. If things get out of hand, don't be afraid to ask for help. Many law-enforcement families feel ashamed to admit that they are struggling; they don't want to show what others might perceive as weakness. This is something that needs to change, so that we support each other instead of judging each other."

"Sometimes it's important to allow your first-responder mate to reach a conclusion himself. For example, I will ask something like 'When's the last

time you saw or spoke with…?' and add the name of a friend who's not a first responder. That way it doesn't come across as being negative, and he will come to his own conclusion that it has been a long time. I will then agree with him and reinforce the thought with a positive memory of that friendship, adding that I miss spending time with that person. Demanding that your mate stop changing or that he go back to 'what he used to be' closes all lines of communication."

"If the change happens to be destructive, you have to be straightforward and say it like it is. In that scenario, be blunt and direct, and do not enable the destructive or inappropriate behavior to continue. Yes, your mate's job is terribly stressful and daunting, but that clearly does not give him a pass to treat you disrespectfully or be involved in destructive, unhealthy behaviors."

How Do You Nurture Your Spirit and Sustain Your Emotional and Spiritual Wellness So You Can Nurture Your First-Responder Spouse?

"Remember that only you can make yourself happy. You are responsible for your own happiness, especially in a first-responder marriage. So many times in your marriage you will be stood up, let down, or disappointed, and none of these incidents will be personal or intentional. That's just the nature of your mate's profession. Try to always focus on the positive — the good things, rather than the bad."

"I highly recommend joining a spouse support group or starting one of your own. I also recommend reading Emotional Survival for Law Enforcement *by Kevin Gilmartin and* I Love a Cop *by Ellen Kirschman."*

"Confidence and independence are important qualities in any healthy individual and will serve you well as the spouse of an officer. It will be very difficult for you if you feel like you always have to be at your mate's side and you need his approval for things. It is important to find a passion or a hobby and to keep yourself busy. And it's important to go to events and get together with family and friends alone, rather than not going at all."

How Can You Start a Spouse Support Group, and Why Should You Do It?

"Having a spouse support group can save marriages. Many first-responder life partners rely on friends, family, and church for support to deal with the absence of their mates. However, as helpful as these resources can be, they can never offer the same kind of support and understanding that a spouse support group offers. It is invaluable to be able to talk with people who are in the same situation, who experience the same frustrations and issues as you do — those who know what it is like to have to celebrate Christmas on December 27 or Mother's Day on a Tuesday."

"Having such a spouse support group allows us to share experiences and ideas that help us understand and grow as wives, mothers, and women. It helps us to know that we are not alone and that it can be done. We motivate each other to work hard and to support our life partners. The group also gives us an avenue to vent, allowing us to get our feelings of frustration out without burdening our husbands and causing unnecessary tension in our marriages and families."

"Establishing a spouse support group starts with a group of people who have a common goal. The word can be spread through word of mouth by peers, first-responder associations or unions, and the agency's administration. Support groups can stay connected through social networks, such as a private Facebook page, email, and monthly events and meetings. Meeting regularly is important so that you stay connected and provide support to all members. Find similar groups online and reach out to them. They can answer most of your questions and assist your group in getting established."

"Once you have established a core group of members, decide what you want to accomplish and how. You can assign specific tasks within the group, such as establishing a website, liaising with police departments in the area, and setting up a group of mentor spouses who are available through email to help with personal issues that are to be kept confidential. There may also be an assigned crisis coordinator who provides information to the main group when critical incidents occur, so that the group

can avoid getting false reports from media sources. Other assignments may include coordinating training events, gathering resources for the group, and providing training and resources regarding PTSD, as well as coordinating social events and gatherings."

A supportive partner is something precious; it is your responsibility as a first responder to do everything possible to stay connected and engaged with your spouse. When you come home, put the job in the back of your mind and tune in to your present role as a husband, wife, mother, father, coach, friend, or other roles you have apart from your work life. This includes never taking them for granted, never forgetting how difficult it is for them to be married to an emergency first responder. Your marriage is not all about you and what you need because of your profession; it is mostly about being loving and supportive so that your partner will, in turn, be there for you. Be engaged with them when you are home. Don't become isolated, distant, disengaged, or reclusive. Show them that they matter, and be present with them.

Life partners of first responders often develop fears and debilitating anxieties that can even potentially lead to PTSD symptoms. Emotional pain from fear can imperil a spouse's ability to care for and support their mate and even to function.

When first responders experience trauma, their spouses may develop their own stress symptoms, including sleeplessness, severe anxieties and fears, grief, poor concentration, uncontrollable crying, serious separation anxiety, excessive thinking, hypervigilance, extreme mood swings, the sense of having no control over circumstances, the feeling of being on an emotional roller coaster, or a sense of impending misfortune. Spouses tend to suppress such feelings, not wanting to worry their first-responder mates. Hiding their own emotional pain can lead to spouses developing much more serious secondary PTSD symptoms.

The principles illustrated throughout this book are just as

effective for the life partners of those first responders who have undergone critical incidents or who are suffering from the acute stress and trauma of the job. Applying the principles in this book to protect, nurture, and sustain their own spirits can be very helpful for spouses. It is essential that life partners of first responders do not neglect themselves, and that they work to sustain and nurture their own spirits. Often spouses try to be strong and independent as they selflessly support and care for their first-responder partners. They don't want to do anything that may upset or worry their mates. But in so doing they can lose sight of their own needs and can find themselves suffering inside. Spouses cannot best support their mates if they neglect themselves and are suffering in silence. Often peer-support teams and resources available to the first-responder mate are also available to their life partners. Make sure you have the contact information for their peer-support team and resources to call upon when you need their help.

It is essential for spouses to find those moments when they can share their emotions and fears with their first-responder mates. And it's important for first responders to hear what their spouses are going through, so that they don't overlook how their jobs affect their families. Talking with a therapist trained in trauma or to a spouse support group is also extremely helpful for spouses. It's important for spouses to learn that their fears, anxieties, and emotional pain are not unique to them, and they can learn from others who have developed effective coping mechanisms.

Self-Awareness Questions to Improve
Your Most Meaningful Relationships

In what ways do you enhance, strengthen, and support your marriage (or other life partnership)? What do you say or do that is negative and potentially harmful to this relationship?

This is a serious question that both you and your mate should periodically ask yourselves in order to do everything you can to strengthen and enhance your relationship. It's vital to be aware of what you are doing, or are not doing, and ways you can improve. Otherwise, you will likely find yourself wearing blinders, not knowing or understanding how your work harms your most important relationship.

Be proactive about showing your life partner and family every day that they are the most important thing in your life. Not by words, but by your actions. What more can you do to show them how much they matter to you?

Have you ever asked your life partner what they needed from you to help them deal with how the job affects the relationship?

Sit them down and ask, then tell them what you need from them. This conversation should occur at least once a year, preferably more often.

Also, ask your life partner (or a close friend if you are single) in what ways they believe you have changed over the years. Tell them it is essential for them to give you feedback whenever they sense that you are not being yourself or are changing in any way.

In the event of a major critical or traumatic incident at work, how would you like your partner to support, comfort, and help you?

Imagine you have been involved in something traumatic that has really bothered you. How would you like your partner to support, comfort, and help you? Prepare your partner by telling them this information before such an incident happens.

How can you more effectively allow your life partner to be the pillar of support who will help nurture and sustain you?

Our life partners need to feel a part of our life, work, and wellness. Tell them what is helpful to you, but allow them to care for and support you in their own unique way. Let them know when you are dealing with something inside. They don't need to know the details, but they do need and deserve to know how you are and what they can do for you. Share with them, and express yourself to them, so they can help nurture you. Communicate honestly, lovingly, and openly.

Chapter Eleven

EFFECTIVE USE
OF CHAPLAIN SERVICES

I don't know what your destiny will be,
but one thing I know: the only ones among you who will be
really happy are those who will have sought
and found how to serve.

— ALBERT SCHWEITZER

*Darren Turner became a chaplain to serve God and help those
in need. In 2007, after only a few months as a battalion chaplain for the US Army's Thirtieth Infantry Regiment, Darren
was sent to Baghdad to serve the one thousand soldiers in his
battalion for fifteen months during the height of the surge in
the Iraq War. His soldiers faced an invisible but lethal enemy
in booby-trapped houses, concealed snipers, and roads laced
with massive bombs. As the sole chaplain for a thousand men
and women, he, too, absorbed all that befell them. He shared
in their absolute joy — and in horrific tragedy. Darren was
charged with the solemn responsibility of acting as a salve for
their scarred souls.*

The needs expressed to Darren seemed endless. He was a

soldier on the battlefield, a counselor behind closed doors, a friend — even a father figure — to these men and women. He was also a tireless, compassionate man who worked endless hours to comfort the grieving, heal the souls of the suffering, and inspire and give hope to those searching within.

Darren recognized the needs his soldiers would have after witnessing the horrors of combat and after losing so many friends. He gave himself unceasingly to providing comfort, support, and understanding to them. And as it turned out, the ghosts of Iraq would haunt not only his soldiers but Darren as well. After his fifteen-month deployment, Darren returned home to face all the same problems he had counseled his soldiers about: anger, depression, stress, PTSD, emotional suffering, and — most important for him — how to preserve relationships with loved ones.

At first, seemingly from nowhere, anger and then rage boiled inside him. As he tried to adjust to being home, the anger began to surface. Darren took it out on his wife, Heather, who had trouble understanding what her husband had become. Darren would later say, "I lost a lot of guys in Iraq, and I didn't take care of my soul while I was there." Little things like how to arrange dishes in the dishwasher became big fights between Darren and Heather. More important things like Heather's life plans became small issues that her husband mocked, derided, or discounted because they didn't fit with his plans.

Darren didn't realize how angry and self-centered he had become until Heather told him one day, "You're no longer welcome in our house." Suddenly, he was about to lose his wife and three young children. He had helped rescue many soldiers in similar circumstances, and now he discovered that he was not immune to suffering and losing himself.

Heather told Darren that he was disengaged, impatient,

distant, and unfeeling — that he was not the man she had married. She wanted the two of them to seek counseling. But Darren, the sought-after counselor himself, refused, insisting that Heather was the one who had issues. Darren had become extremely selfish and tried to obsessively control everyone and everything concerning him. A short time later the couple separated.

Darren soon resigned from the chaplaincy and took a job in sales at Home Depot. He struggled to keep from losing his wife — and his faith. Four months later, Darren and Heather reconciled. Through spending time alone, Darren had come to terms with how he was behaving and how his service had changed him. He could now begin to heal. With a renewed spirit and the insight he gained from his personal trials and healing, Darren returned to the army as a chaplain to continue to serve and heal others.

Now [in 2015] Darren is stationed in Afghanistan, where he counsels soldiers who are about to return home from the war. He works to keep them connected with their loved ones back home, often allowing them to use his own personal cell phone to call home from the field. Darren is convinced that distance from one's family can trigger a breakdown, especially when a soldier is coping with injuries and combat stress. Darren's ministry offers hope — the hope and dream of healing. For more on Chaplain Darren Turner, read the book Chaplain Turner's War *by Moni Basu.*

Chaplains are ordained professional clergy, and they have extensive training and experience in counseling, listening, and advising on critical issues and personal problems, in ways specific to your needs as a first responder. Ever since the American Revolutionary War, chaplains have selflessly served and made sacrifices for the military in combat. Their devoted service to the armed forces, as well as to police, fire personnel, medics, and hospitals, has supported, strengthened, healed, inspired, and uplifted the spirits of our emergency first responders. Countless heroic chaplains have always put the needs of those they serve first — sometimes at the expense of their own lives.

The invaluable, life-sustaining services chaplains offer are, however, useful only if you make an effort to become acquainted with them and to give them a chance. A chaplain's sole purpose for being a part of your agency is to serve, comfort, aid, and assist you in whatever capacity you need.

Chaplain programs in law enforcement have existed for decades, but far too few law-enforcement organizations and other first-responder agencies utilize this vitally important component of officer wellness and survival. A trained chaplain is specially selected by your agency to become an integral part of the organization and its culture. The chaplain is a resource available 24/7 to assist first responders in any circumstance.

A chaplain program is a volunteer unit created to provide nondenominational mental, emotional, and spiritual support to agency personnel, to their families, and to victims of crimes and tragedies in the community. Chaplains are qualified, specifically trained, and selected professional clergy who provide essential counsel and assistance when called upon. They absolutely do not promote any specific religious doctrine and, in fact, are prohibited from doing so. Instead they offer ecumenical service to provide a critically needed resource.

All types of agencies can benefit from the help of chaplains, who can aid in many ways. They can serve by regularly riding along with first responders on duty; by visiting dispatchers, fire personnel, paramedics, or military personnel at work; by visiting them while they're sick or injured, whether at the hospital or at home; by participating in critical-incident stress management debriefings; and by performing wedding and funeral services, ceremonial invocations and benedictions at agency functions, and any other appropriate services that you may seek. They also assist first responders by helping with death notifications and offer immediate support and assistance to victims and relatives of victims of violent crimes, accidents, suicides, or other tragedies.

Chaplains empathetically enter into the crisis, trauma, and suffering that you or others may be experiencing, and they do so without discrimination toward any race, religion, or creed. They walk with emergency first responders in a ministry of purpose, presence, and peace. Their focus is solely upon assisting you and those who are suffering in any way toward restored emotional, mental, and spiritual wellness.

Exactly how chaplains may aid others depends on whatever is needed to comfort and assist those involved in a wide variety of situations. They might do something as small as getting a bottle of water for a firefighter or as wrenching as providing death notifications and ministering to grieving family members. They might also serve by disseminating resources, helping with CPR, offering an unbiased listening ear, running the car computer, prepping meals for officers involved in a long-term SWAT incident, answering questions at your initiation, providing marriage/relationship and grief counseling, taking notes when the computer goes down, serving as an extra set of eyes on a traffic stop, or anything else you may need in order to do your job.

The confidentiality of the counseling and support services that a chaplain program offers to first responders is legally protected — equal to their seeing a professional psychologist or psychiatrist. This is critical. Unless you disclose that you have been involved in a crime or something else for which the law mandates reporting, any conversation you have with a chaplain is legally confidential. The chief of police cannot order a chaplain to divulge information learned in a conversation. First responders love the confidentiality aspect of chaplain services.

Requirements for Effective Chaplain Services

Not every member of the clergy can become an effective chaplain for first responders. In fact, most clergy are not a good fit. As peer-support teams or first responders establish a chaplain service program, they must recognize that a prospective chaplain should have a special interest in and understanding of the specific profession, coupled with the ability to become a part of the culture. The chaplain must be able to relate to the first responders not necessarily as a clergyperson but as a confidential resource there solely for the well-being of his or her charges. For information about becoming a chaplain and training, see the International Conference of Police Chaplains website: www.icpc4cops.org.

It's important for current or prospective chaplains to understand that a chaplain program is never a vehicle for proselytizing or converting first responders to one particular religious belief. Instead, chaplains respect each employee and each employee's own spiritual viewpoint. A chaplain serves employees who have no spiritual beliefs by supporting them according to their needs, just as they would support employees who have strong religious viewpoints. Chaplains might talk of spiritual matters when first responders open the door by asking the chaplain questions about spirituality or otherwise bringing up the issue on their own. Chaplains are trained to use an employee's own beliefs to benefit and support the employee, regardless of the chaplain's personal background or beliefs. In other words, chaplains should understand that they are servants first and foremost, and be ecumenical in their conversations. They listen first, seek to learn, and then talk. They are a "guest" in the first responder's "house" and should act respectfully and humbly at all times in order to be most effective. If they don't, they should be discouraged, or prevented, from volunteering further.

Important Information for Starting a Chaplain Service Program

A first-responder chaplain should be an ecclesiastically certified person in good standing and endorsed for law-enforcement (first-responder) chaplaincy by a recognized religious body, with five years' experience in ministry. He or she should be carefully screened by the first-responder agency, including a thorough background check. The chaplain should be available to serve on a twenty-four-hour, on-call basis.

A first-responder chaplain should manifest a broad base of experience in professional ministry, emotional stability, and personal flexibility, as well as be tactful and considerate in approaching all people, regardless of race, sex, beliefs, or religion. He or she should also be willing to receive training that enhances efficiency in meeting and dealing with people in crisis and should be familiar with medical, psychiatric, and other supportive resources in the community.

Your chaplain program should have clearly defined department instructions or rules and regulations. (To obtain the La Mesa Police Department's Chaplain Program Standard Operating Procedures, email me at dwillis1121@yahoo.com.)

The selection of the right chaplain is critical in establishing an effective chaplain program, and so a detailed process should be established for selecting your chaplain. Potential interview questions for prospective chaplains could include the following:

- How do you see your role as a chaplain for our agency?
- What is your purpose as a chaplain, and how will you be effective?
- Explain the difference between clergy and a chaplain.
- What is your priority and main focus as a chaplain — the needs of the officer (or first responder) or your religious beliefs?
- Why do you want to become a chaplain?
- How will you build rapport with an officer (or first responder)?
- How long have you been involved in counseling, and are you willing to counsel all people in the department, regardless of their beliefs?
- What assets do you bring to the agency?
- What resources are available to you from the community?
- Have you ever applied to another agency as a chaplain? What were the results?

There are professional organizations that offer information, training, and guidelines to chaplains for first responders. The following are some of the better ones:

- International Conference of Police Chaplains, www.icpc4 cops.org
- CAREForce, www.careforce.us
- International Critical Incident Stress Foundation, https:// icisf.org

Issues Involving Chaplains

If a selected chaplain subsequently does not fit in or is not effective, you should report it immediately to the person who oversees the chaplain program so that corrective action can be taken. A number of possible issues require that chaplains be monitored. For instance, chaplains need certain training to ensure that they understand their specific role as a chaplain first and foremost, rather than as a clergyperson. They need to clearly understand their purpose and limitations as defined in the agency's rules and regulations. A chaplain who is reticent about training should be dismissed.

Another potential issue is when a chaplain becomes uninvolved. Chaplains must commit to a certain number of hours each month, as specified in the agency's rules and regulations. If a chaplain is rarely present, distrust tends to develop. Why would a first responder open up to a chaplain who is not expected to be there next week or next month? If a chaplain consistently fails to put in the minimum amount of time required, he or she should be dismissed.

Confidentiality might potentially be an issue as well. If a chaplain ever breaks confidence in any way, other than for a legally mandated reason, that chaplain must be reported and dismissed immediately in order to preserve the chaplain program.

Finally, chaplains, like their first-responder charges, are susceptible to burnout as a result of cumulative stress or specific incidents that cause mental, emotional, or spiritual trauma. They should be allowed to access counseling services from the agency, access the peer-support team, participate in a critical-incident stress management debriefing, and take time off when needed. Just as the chaplain watches out for the first responders, someone needs to watch for any signs of burnout in the chaplain.

A Chaplain's Personal Experience in Serving Others

The Reverend Chuck Price has been a chaplain with the San Diego Police and El Cajon Police Departments for over twenty years.

He has had countless experiences of officers opening up to him, asking for professional and personal counseling, marriage and family counseling, and support of all other kinds. He has received numerous calls in the middle of the night from officers who have just experienced something traumatic or are in need of spiritual support. He has witnessed, many times over, the invaluable role an effective chaplain can play in the wellness and emotional survival of first responders. The following firsthand experiences of the Reverend Price demonstrate just how necessary a chaplain can be to you and your colleagues.

You never know what you are going to be asked to do for the officers. Whatever it was, I did it, and my actions have always been very much appreciated. I see firsthand how helpful and comforting a chaplain can be.

The first and second times I was called to assist involved motorcycle officers who had been killed in the line of duty. I did an immense amount of counseling for the family members and many officers. I also officiated at both funerals. I am still friends with officers from both of those incidents and even performed the wedding of the partner of one of the deceased officers.

Once I was asked by a newer officer if "you guys [chaplains] do weddings." I ended up riding with the officer soon after that, meeting his fiancée, and conducting their premarital counseling. Both their families had my wife and me over for dinner. I performed the wedding ceremony, and we have remained good friends to this day.

An officer once asked me if I could come by the station sometime. Apparently, he wanted to talk with me about something. I met the officer after lineup, and he began to tell me about the death of the love of his life — his wife of many years. She had recently died of cancer. This officer was in deep grief, as would be expected. He was perhaps the saddest person I have ever met. I did my best to comfort him, and I followed up with him over the next year. He called me several times along the way; we would meet and talk about how he was suffering, and I listened and supported him. For a long time, however, nothing changed. He was grieving deeply, but on the outside he appeared to be functioning like any other officer. Recently I got a call from him. He wanted to let me know that he was out of his depression and doing well.

One night I received a call from a lieutenant who asked if I was available to respond immediately to a call where an infant had died from sudden infant death syndrome while sleeping. When I arrived at the scene, the lieutenant briefed me and pointed to a patrol car where the primary officer was typing his report. I got in the car with the officer, whom I had ridden with many times before, and began to evaluate how he was doing. After some time, I could see that he was doing all right with what had happened, and I got out and went to the home, where other officers were waiting for the medical examiner.

The family members were grieving terribly but, at the same time, were estranged from each other. I engaged with each person separately and was able to offer them all some support and care during their time of shock and immediate grief. After the incident, I followed up with all the officers who had been on the scene, to ensure they were doing well.

Three weeks later I was riding with the officer who had performed CPR on the baby in this incident. The same lieutenant who had asked me to come help with that earlier incident now asked us to come back to the station. While we were finishing a call and getting ready to return to the station, another call came over the radio about a nonbreathing baby. We were the closest unit. We arrived first on the scene and immediately went to where the baby was sitting in a little sling chair.

I followed the officer in and, after a quick assessment, he notified the dispatcher that the baby was dead. We backed out of the room, and the officer preserved the scene. As the officer began his investigation, I went into counseling mode with the housemates of the parents and, eventually, the mother and father. I was given the task of caring for the mom and dad while the investigation ensued.

Many hours later we cleared the scene and went back to the station. The next day I received a call letting me know that the baby had been murdered. I provided support to the officer involved and listened to him as he tried to make sense of this senseless murder.

I have attended both the state and national memorials held for law-enforcement officers in Sacramento and Washington, DC. While at each of the memorials, I connected with officers that I had previously not known and provided grief counseling. This happened simply because I was present and was paying attention. I also interacted with the families of both and have stayed in touch with members of each family since.

I once received a call from a captain telling me that an officer had committed suicide. I knew the officer. I rushed to the scene, which was the officer's house. I met the deceased officer's wife, three kids, and in-laws and the officers who had served with him. I ended up counseling them all over the following several weeks. I officiated at the officer's funeral and have stayed in touch with his wife. I recently attended a Survivors of Suicide Loss meeting with her.

I have lost count of the number of times that I have done critical-incident stress management debriefings, which have ranged from instances regarding an incident that happened *a few weeks earlier with a single officer in a car to ones that happened almost two decades earlier. I do this intuitively, recognizing that something is disturbing them, and because I care about traumatic times early in their careers that have never been processed, from back when wellness was not much on the radar. These incidents can still be causing significant emotional wounds.*

Advice for Other Chaplains from Reverend Price

In order to connect with first responders, a chaplain must spend time consistently at the agency and with officers. If they see you around all the time, and you are not intrusive in any way, you might have a chance to help them. Be yourself. Let them get to know you. Far more importantly, ask nonintrusive questions so you can get to know them. Be interested not only in how they do their job but also in who they are outside of work. Don't try to be a cop or act like you know what you clearly don't know about their job. Be an active listener and learner — always. Get to know their culture and find your place in it.

Love, care for, and support them right where they are. Do not ever try to change them. Never make the passenger seat your bully pulpit to correct someone's language, fix what you think might be broken, or question the way they do their job. You are in their world and, normally, not by invitation. You are invading their "office" and interrupting their routine. The chaplain is not only an outsider but also, on top of that, some kind of religious person who has no idea what their faith background (if any) is.

Have a sense of humor. First responders often use dark humor to cope with uncomfortable situations and horrible crime scenes. Officers may question the "real" reason why you are there. Be prepared to answer. Don't take things personally, even if you would be offended if the same thing were said to you in your place of worship, because you are not there and they are not bound by the rules of your faith.

Don't lead with questions about faith or belief. Explain what your role is as a chaplain and why you're there — to support and care for them as they may need. If an officer initiates a discussion on religion or faith, then feel free to talk about it. But don't be the one to bring it up. And if they don't... that's perfectly all right. You are there solely to support and care for them according to their needs and wants — nothing else.

Always be credible and trustworthy. First responders always talk to each other. At the end of a shift, the officer you rode with will be asked how it went. If you connected with a single officer on a ride-along, that officer will become a building block of your credibility. First responders are by nature extremely distrustful. They will be checking you out from the time you arrive until the time you leave; and they will continue to do so until they know they can trust you. You are an outsider. Take your time, be patient, be humble, and build their trust.

Learn to feel compassion for those who are arrested, and be at peace with their arrest. Try to understand how compassionate an arrest actually is, since the officer is preventing further victimization as well as providing a negative consequence that may ultimately serve to change the arrestee's criminal and/or self-destructive behavior. Justice, compassion, and peace involve preventing people from harming themselves or others.

I have experienced countless times the significant ways an effective chaplain can benefit a first responder and an agency. I know we have assisted in healing and in saving careers, marriages, and even lives. A chaplain is a trained and caring server who is involved with the first-responder community, and who provides the kind of support and assistance that is not available to them elsewhere.

Self-Awareness Questions Regarding Seeking Help

Would you ever use the services of a chaplain? If not, why not? Are there any past experiences in your personal or professional life in which you should have sought the advice, support, and counsel of a chaplain?

Try to get to know the chaplain for your agency. Once you have gotten to know them, talk with them about an experience you have had where you may need some advice, or just someone to listen to you, either personally or professionally. As clergy, chaplains deal with people's problems, issues, and trauma all the time. They can truly be a trusted resource for you if you understand their role and use their services to benefit you.

Is there anything pertaining to your beliefs and how you view yourself that would prevent you from ever seeking assistance from a professional?

You have nothing to lose by engaging with a chaplain. If you do so and feel afterward that they were not helpful, at least you made an effort. More likely, you will find that talking with a chaplain, who is sincerely there solely to help and assist you, will benefit you.

Chapter Twelve

ONE OFFICER'S SURVIVAL STORY

Everything can be taken from a person but one thing:
the last of human freedoms — to choose one's attitude
in any given set of circumstances, to choose one's own way.
— Viktor E. Frankl

In years past, whenever officers at my station were involved in
critical incidents, they were on their own. There was no wellness
program or peer-support team to turn to for help. There was no
critical-incident stress management debriefing; in fact, there was
nothing in the way of support or assistance to help an officer process trauma. Sometimes officers processed the incident all right
on their own, but more often than not, they suffered. Without
training in how to prepare for and mitigate the effects of a critical
incident, officers were left to suffer alone and hope for the best.

More than a year after the agency implemented the BeSTOW
philosophy, Officer Tim Purdy was involved in a life-or-death situation. His experience offered the perfect test case: Had my department changed at all? Officer Purdy describes how the actions

of peers and supervisors, along with an active wellness program and the BeSTOW philosophy, can actually save a career and potentially a life. He also details his PTSD and how the treatment therapy of EMDR gave him his life back.

August 19, 2011, was just another hot, muggy Friday night that I spent working patrol. Everything was going along as expected during the shift, which consisted of six officers and one sergeant, all on patrol in their own cars. Then, just after midnight, I received my next call: a man was reported walking in the street in a residential neighborhood carrying a gun. Something in the dispatcher's voice told me this was not going to be an ordinary call. Immediately, something just didn't feel right.

While I was driving to the location and coordinating my approach with the other responding units and the sergeant, the dispatcher informed us that additional 911 calls were coming in about the man with the gun. I can still clearly recall the alarm in the dispatcher's voice as she radioed, "We are now receiving numerous calls confirming the man has a shotgun and is walking in the middle of the street." We were headed for a very quiet residential street where nothing ever happened. The dispatcher's trembling voice foreshadowed the horror we were all about to experience as she continued, "The suspect is a parolee who just threatened to kill his wife and children."

I thought this call could be seriously life threatening for everyone involved, including my brother officers and myself. I didn't think my heart could beat any faster, and I had to really focus on catching my breath as I arrived at the staging point, about a block away from where the suspect was last seen. My fellow officers and I gathered together and quickly talked with each other to devise a plan. We then all began tactically walking toward the darkened area where the suspect was last seen, carefully approaching by using parked cars as our cover. I could feel my heart pounding in my chest faster and faster as we walked closer to the area. We had no way of knowing if we were about to be targets for a murderer.

We were searching everywhere and listening for something, anything, that would tell us where the man with the rifle was. It was eerily quiet — no screams, no yelling, just silence and darkness. Was he hiding somewhere in the shadows, waiting to ambush us? Had he already killed his family?

As we continued to approach the darkened area, suddenly a man's yell pierced the quiet. I walked toward the middle of the street, hands clenching my gun, as my partners and best friends, who were directly across from me, stealthily approached from behind parked cars along both sides of the street. One dim streetlamp illuminated a small area just ahead of us, and I saw a man standing beneath it, yelling. Immediately I noticed he had something in his hand, but I could not tell what it was. I shone my flashlight on the suspect for a couple of seconds and confirmed that in his left hand he was carrying a shotgun that was pointing toward the ground.

Someone yelled, "He's got a gun! Get to cover!" I could now clearly see the suspect approximately twenty feet in front of me. (It was later determined that I was around twenty-five yards away, but at the time it seemed much closer.) The suspect was still yelling, but I could not understand what he was saying. I began shouting, "Police! Drop the gun!" and praying that he would comply.

As my fellow officers and I continued to yell for the suspect to put down the shotgun, I noticed one of the neighbors standing on his front patio. The neighbor was calling out to the suspect and attempting to calm him down. We later learned that they did in fact know each other. At that moment everything changed.

I can see it all so clearly in my mind. We continued to yell for the suspect to put down the shotgun, not knowing whether he had just killed or seriously injured his family. We had to take care of this suspect and get to the family, all of whom at that moment could be slowly dying or already be dead.

The suspect suddenly turned his body toward my partners. I don't think he was aware of my location at that point, but he definitely knew where two of my best friends were — taking cover behind a parked car. The suspect then raised the shotgun with his right hand, pointing it toward the sky. I still get chilled to this day when I remember what I heard next — the distinctive sound of the suspect racking a round into the shotgun chamber, preparing it to be fired. That racking sound was the loudest thing I heard; the noise seemed to echo throughout the neighborhood.

I could not believe this was happening. Why was this guy not listening to us? I continued yelling for the suspect to put down the shotgun, but he chose to level that shotgun instead and point it directly at my partners. It was the most terrifying moment I have ever experienced.

In fear for my partners' lives, I fired my duty handgun at the suspect. I can still see the flash from the barrel. When I fired it, everything slowed down. It was as if it were happening in slow motion. I saw the suspect's body begin to drop. Several more bullets, fired by my partners, began striking his body, also seemingly in slow motion. We had all fired almost simultaneously. The noise was so loud that the gunshots were recorded on the 911 audiotapes as a witness continued speaking with the dispatcher from inside his home, but I hadn't heard any of the shots. Every movement seemed unreal to me, but the few *seconds after the suspect had been put down will remain in my mind for the rest of my life.*

I remember looking over after several seconds and seeing both of my partners. I yelled at them, asking if they were all right. They each replied with a "Yes." A few more seconds went by and I was able to confirm that all my partners were safe. I radioed that shots had been fired and the suspect was down. Now I had to get my mindset back, because I knew we still had to take the suspect into custody, but I didn't know for sure if he was still a threat. We all began communicating from behind cover and then started moving in toward the downed suspect.

The suspect had dropped the shotgun after being shot, and it was still lying at his feet. I approached the suspect first as other officers kicked the shotgun away from him. I remember the suspect's face so clearly. His eyes were wide open, and they had rolled up toward the top of his head, showing mostly the whites. Blood surrounded his entire body, and the pool grew larger and larger. This sight was something I would see over and over again in my mind for a long time.

In any first-responder role, if you see blood you automatically know to put on gloves. I still do not know why I didn't put gloves on my hands before touching the suspect's body. I can't explain why, but I didn't follow procedure. I grabbed the suspect's arm and began pulling him over on his side. I remember his arm feeling slick and sticky from all the blood. There was blood everywhere.

As I rolled the suspect over onto his side I could hear the last little bit of air come out of his mouth, spattering blood on my arm. I had to place my hand on his back in order to get his body to turn over. I could feel my hand going into his wounds, the bleeding holes in his body, as I began pushing him onto his stomach. My hands kept slipping in blood from his arms as I *attempted to place him in handcuffs. I remember getting angry at him for making me have to do this, but I continued to do my job. I had never touched a dead man before — a man I had just helped kill.*

The suspect was placed in handcuffs and first aid was rendered to him. I knew he was dead, but I also knew it was not over. I knew we had to find the suspect's family. We had to find out what had happened and whether anyone else was injured. I didn't know if his wife or kids, if they were still alive, had witnessed the shooting and possibly wanted to retaliate against us. The thought raced through my mind that there could be other suspects as well. I knew I had to collect myself and continue doing my job.

I grabbed one of my partners and told my sergeant we were going to find out what had occurred and check the reporting party's residence. I didn't think twice about it. I was not going to stop until I found the family and knew everyone was safe.

While approaching the suspect's house, which stood nearby, I heard a woman screaming. I saw her come out of a house with her arms wide open, running directly toward me. I later learned that this was one of the witnesses who had first seen the suspect with the shotgun. I noticed she was crying and I identified myself as a police officer. She came directly up to me, still screaming, "He has a gun! Where are the kids?"

I asked her if she could tell me which house belonged to the family and she said it was directly across the street. The last thing I remember her saying was "Oh my God, where are the kids?" I thought for sure I was about to walk into a bloody, grisly scene of death.

I told the neighbor to go back inside her home and stay there. I turned and looked across the street at the suspect's house. The front door was open and several lights were on, but it was completely quiet inside — eerily quiet. I thought the man's entire family was probably dead. I gathered myself again, bracing myself, knowing I still had to do my job. I radioed that I needed another officer in order to clear the suspect's house. Three of us entered the home, and I remember how we braced ourselves as we entered every room, thinking we were going to find a family shot to death. But we didn't. The house was empty.

When we came out of the home, I heard someone say, "The family is inside my house, officer." It was the suspect's neighbor. The family had run over to his house a few seconds after the suspect walked outside with the shotgun. The neighbor informed me that the suspect's wife was inside his living room and the two small children were asleep in the back bedroom. At least they had not seen us kill their father.

While walking toward the front door I could feel the dry, sticky blood on my hands. Inside, I saw the suspect's wife sitting on the sofa. I didn't want her to see my hands so I placed them down by my side as I asked, "Are you injured at all?" She looked at me and said, "I'm okay. He just went crazy." I asked where her children were and told her I wanted to make sure they were all right. She told me the kids were sleeping in a room down the hall. I remember running toward the bedroom; I had to see them.

My hand was completely covered in blood as I turned the door handle, smearing it badly. I opened the door and could see two small children sleeping in the bed. I started to walk back out of the room when the little girl, who was sleeping with her brother, sat up, with her sweet, innocent face, and said, "Hi." I said "Hi" back. The little girl asked, "Where is my daddy?" I can still see those beautiful little eyes staring up at me as she asked about her daddy, whom I had just killed. I didn't know *what to say. The feeling that came over me then was something I have never experienced before as a police officer. This little girl, who had no idea what had just happened, was asking me about her father. What could I possibly say to her? I walked over to her bedside, still hiding my hands covered in her father's blood. I told her everything was going to be okay. "Just go ahead and go back to sleep." I still can see that little girl's face smiling at me as she put her head back down and wrapped her arm over the top of her brother. I closed the bedroom door and walked back to the living room.*

I could feel the sticky blood on my hands, and I could see blood on my duty weapon and my flashlight. I was covered in blood. When I spoke on my radio microphone I could feel the blood there as well. But I never stopped thinking about my objective, and continued doing my job. I spoke again to the suspect's wife in the living room. She wasn't crying, but I could tell she was scared. I didn't want her to see my hands, but unfortunately she did. The first thing out of her mouth when she saw me was "Did someone get hurt? You have blood on your hands." Again I had to think quickly and responded by telling her that someone had been injured, but I didn't know how badly.

By this time I felt an urgent need to get out of that house. My heart beat faster as I spoke to the suspect's wife. I confirmed again that she was not injured and told her to please stay inside the house, that another officer would return for her soon. I could not get out of that residence fast enough. I felt like my heart was going to break in half; it ached like it had never before or has since.

I returned to the scene of the shooting and told my sergeant what I had learned. The light from that one streetlamp continued to shine down on the large pool of blood encircling the suspect's body, highlighting his intestines, which one of the bullets had perforated.

A short time later my chain of command started to arrive on the scene. Our wellness program was set into motion nearly from the beginning. I had no idea how much it would eventually mean to me and my wife. It was obvious that the primary concern of everyone — from the chief to the captains and lieutenants and everyone else — was the well-being of my partners and me. They would show us great consideration in everything they did, not only that night but also for months to come. At that moment I was afraid. I had no idea what to expect or what was going to happen; but I immediately felt they would be there for me.

As we walked away, we had to walk past the suspect's body. I remember looking at his body one more time as I walked by. His eyes were still open, blood trickling from his gaping mouth, and I knew for sure he was dead. It wasn't until that moment that I finally knew it was really over. I felt a tremendous load fall from my shoulders, and my body ached as if I had just run twenty miles. I knew then that we were finally all safe.

As we continued walking I started to sweat, and I suddenly experienced a shortness of breath. I almost felt as if I were about to fall to the ground, but I managed to continue standing. My lieutenant took my arm and asked me if I was all right. I told him, "No. I'm not okay. I don't know what's going on with me, but I'm not okay." A serious panic attack had hit me, although I didn't realize it. I had no idea what was happening to me, and the feelings terrified me.

Fortunately, the command staff and, it seemed, the entire police department stepped up and started doing what they could to take care of all of us. My lieutenant asked, "Do you want to ride back with me?" Just being asked to ride back to the station with him was a great comfort to me; it proved to be a significant help to me, something I think about to this very day. Another officer put his arm around me and said, "Let's first go over here to my car so we can clean up some of that blood," which he did.

As·I got in the car with my lieutenant, I felt protected. I could feel my heart rate drop back down as we drove toward the police station. Throughout the ride he continued to talk with me, saying that if I needed anything at all, to just let him know. Once we reached the station, he walked with me to the locker room. He stayed with me for as long as he could and even called my wife to tell her I was all right. My superiors in the department, too, were there for us right from the start.

It was evident that, even though the department was facing a daunting job with the ensuing criminal and administrative investigations that could take months, they had our well-being in mind and would make sure we were well cared for. Just knowing that and seeing how they cared for us as people, not only as officers, made all the difference in our recovery.

Shortly after my partners and I arrived in the locker room, another lieutenant came in and asked for our weapons. He immediately gave us each a new weapon, and I knew this was part of the process. Later, photographs were taken of all of us, individually, along with our duty belts. My partners and I were allowed to remain together in a large conference room, which I was very thankful for, as we conducted interviews privately with our collective attorney. It was another great comfort and relief to be allowed to stay with my brother officers during this process. We were simply told not to talk about the shooting, but that we could remain there with one another. The chief had already called for the president of our police officers' union to be there to help and advise us. Several peer-support team

members arrived to keep us company; they kept asking if there
was anything they could do for us — contact our families, bring
us water or coffee, anything. They had shown up in the middle
of the night to offer their support and assistance in any way
possible. That was a great comfort as well. The peer-support
members were also reaching out to the department's chaplain
so she could join us as well.

I remember being so hungry, and when my captain walked
in the room with bags of Carl's Jr. burgers, it was the best meal
I could have wished for. We hadn't even asked for anything yet.
That was the best burger I'd ever had in my life! This was just
another way my department was taking care of us.

A short time after we ate, the lieutenant overseeing the
investigation entered the conference room. He also happened
to be one of the original coordinators of our wellness program.
He first asked us each again if we were all right and whether we
needed anything at all. He then told us that whatever the investigation showed, everything would be okay — we were a family
and we would be taken care of and supported. He proceeded to
explain the entire investigative process to us, both the criminal
and the administrative investigations. He talked about how we
would have three days off work on administrative leave, and
then we would stay on leave until we were approved by the
police psychologist to return to work or until we felt we were all
right to return. He explained each step of the process and stayed
to answer every question we had. Just having someone tell us
what to expect eased my mind tremendously.

The lieutenant then told us that he would make sure none
of us were interviewed that night. Some of us wanted to be
interviewed to get it over with, knowing that we had nothing
to hide. He insisted that they never conduct interviews of critical incidents the same day or even the next, because to do so

wouldn't be in our best interest. He told us that we would forget many details and that we would begin to remember them after a few days. He wanted to make sure that we would be interviewed only once and that each of us would be able to provide the most detailed information possible. It was only later that I realized this procedure really served us in the best way possible.

Much later I also learned that the command staff back at the scene had held a discussion and ultimately decided to use a barricade screen to obscure the body when we returned to the scene that night. They knew that, as part of the initial investigation, we would be asked to conduct a walk-through — a preliminary, very limited public-safety interview that examined only the basic details of the event: where people had been when they shot their weapons, and so on. The fact that fellow officers made sure I did not have to see the dead man's body again when we went back out there was one of the most compassionate acts my department performed for us.

I knew in my heart that this was a justified shooting. But we had just taken a man's life, so of course thoughts were racing through my mind: maybe this hadn't been a good shooting; maybe I would lose my job or get sued; or, the unthinkable, maybe I would be prosecuted. This shooting also reminded me of a previous incident, when my partner and I had nearly been shot. Whatever I was thinking, the steps the department had taken so far were managing to keep me calm.

I remember thinking over and over that I just wanted to go home and see my wife. I had no idea when I would be allowed to do that, but I needed to see her so badly. After a couple of hours had passed, we were finally informed that the department was letting us go home now and that we would come back three days later to conduct our interviews. They wanted to take care of us and make sure we got rest and spent some time with our loved ones. I can tell you that this decision was incredibly meaningful to me. Words cannot describe it. This was my department taking care of its own.

When I got home my wife was standing at the front door waiting for me. I walked in and we held each other for what seemed like hours. I didn't want to let go of her. I didn't talk to her about what happened. She didn't need me to say anything. She only had to see that I was safe. She only needed to know that I was all right. At the time I couldn't have known that this shooting would put a real strain on our marriage, cause us to fight at times, and cause an uncomfortable distance between us. I didn't know that parts of me and my outlook on life would forever be changed. I didn't know what I needed in order to feel better, so how could she possibly know?

I finally put her to bed and was able to get in the shower. I could still feel the sticky blood on my hands, even though I had long ago washed it all off. When I got in the shower, I noticed that the three small diamonds on my wedding ring were still encased in the suspect's blood. I immediately started scrubbing my ring, and then I started seeing blood on my hands. I scrubbed so hard it felt like my skin was about to come off. No matter how hard I scrubbed, I still kept seeing blood on my hands and going down the drain — even though I knew there couldn't be any. In my mind, the water I was standing in was a pool of blood.

This was the moment when I completely broke down. I could not believe what had happened. I cried for about fifteen minutes, continuing to see blood on my hands that wasn't even there. Was I losing my mind? I didn't want my wife to see me like that; it would really upset her. So I internalized my pain, suppressed it, and got out of the shower. I dried off and entered our bedroom. For the first time that night she asked if I could talk to her about what had happened. I said I didn't want to talk about it and left it at that. We both finally got some sleep, but it would be a long road to overcome what had just happened in our lives. The emotional trauma of being in a life-or-death situation, and of taking another's life — no matter how justified — is a life-altering experience.

The next day I received a call from the department, informing me that we were required by policy to see the department psychologist before we returned to duty. I was given a date for my appointment with the doctor, but I was not looking forward to meeting with him. I absolutely did not want to talk about what had happened. I still couldn't, and didn't want to, talk to my own wife about what had happened. How in the world could I talk to a complete stranger? I felt I could work out my feelings on my own, but I also managed to keep an open mind about the psychologist — at least to a certain point!

So, I met with this psychologist two days after the shooting. At that time I was really having a hard time with everything, trying to put the incident into perspective, trying to make sense of it all. My home life had already been affected in just two short days. I told the psychologist what had happened, and we spoke for about forty-five minutes. When we finished our session, he told me he needed to meet with me again in one week to continue talking. He suggested that I ask my wife to come with me for that meeting, so I brought her along the next time.

The second meeting with this psychologist seemed to leave my wife and me with more questions than when we came in. For whatever reason, I just didn't feel comfortable talking things through with him and was left wondering if I could be sent to see a different psychologist. All I knew was that I was not even remotely close to being ready to return to work and needed to find a psychologist who I felt more comfortable relating to.

The following day I got a phone call from another officer at the department. She was a dear friend of mine and also served on the department's peer-support team. The first thing she asked me was how the meeting had gone with the doctor. I told her what had happened and she immediately said, "Let me call you right back!"

Shortly after hanging up the phone, I received a call from the same investigations lieutenant who had talked with us on the night of the shooting. I explained everything to him and he replied, "We will fix it on our end, and I will call you right back." I can say at this point I felt some relief because the department had already shown me how much they cared and supported us, so I knew he would try to help me now.

Soon afterward I received a phone call from my captain, who told me that they were making arrangements with the human resources department to find another psychologist for me to see and that I should not worry about what had happened with the first doctor. I was told that they only wanted me to take care of myself and my family and that I should not worry about coming back to work until I was ready.

I must say, I was starting to feel guilty for not going back to work. It was extremely hard for me to accept the fact that I needed to speak with a respectable psychologist. Though I felt the need to just get back to work, in my heart I knew I really needed to address this incident. The aftermath of the shooting was already starting to physically and mentally tear me apart, as well as my marriage. I was having dreams about the children in the bedroom and nightmares about the shooting. I was seeing blood everywhere, even when I ate. I never wanted to go outside or be around anyone. I knew if I didn't do something, it very well could be the end of my life. Fortunately, my department's actions played a huge part in helping me make that decision.

I was contacted by the human resources department the same day, and an appointment was made with another doctor that afternoon. My department had stepped up again to take care of its own. Their immediate action was amazing to see and had an immediate calming effect on me. I saw the second doctor, who actually cared about what I had to say. I got the help I needed in therapy and was also able to work out my issues related to a near-shooting incident that had occurred a year earlier. It took several sessions with this doctor, but I knew that talking to her was the best medicine I could receive.

The department continued to call to see how I was doing — even calling my wife to ask how she was doing and what they could do to help. Peer-support team members were calling every day initially, sometimes more than once a day, just to check in and see if I needed anything. They always seemed to be there for my family and me. With their support, along with that of my family and friends, I returned to work about a month and a half later with a clear mind and a healthy body.

One week after the shooting, the peer-support team held a critical-incident stress management debriefing with a department psychologist facilitating. The department chaplain was there as well. This procedure was a mandatory debriefing for anyone who had worked the incident, including dispatchers. My department arranged to have two officers from neighboring agencies who had each been involved in multiple shootings attend the debriefing. Although everyone involved was required to attend, we were not required to talk. This debriefing, especially with the added insight of the visiting officers, was critical to our healing and to processing what had happened.

During our debriefing, another police psychologist held a separate debriefing for the wives of all the involved officers, along with peer-support team members. This was done so that our spouses would have their own forum to discuss how the shooting had affected them and so they could receive training in how to most effectively support their spouses. The spouses' debriefing was an innovative new concept in the wellness program — and it was critical to our overall success.

I can tell you that the actions of my department absolutely saved my career, and that I have since become a member of our SWAT team, a field training officer, and a member of the peer-support team. I was recently promoted to sergeant as well. And I can even say that my department's efforts to take care of me — to show me in so many ways how valued I was and how much they cared about my well-being — likely saved my life. If not for the many fellow officers who took steps to make sure I got the help I needed, I know for sure I would have gone down a dark road toward self-destruction. I can't say with certainty that the outcome would have been suicide, but it might have ended that way. In any case, it would have been a terrible outcome.

All my partners involved in the shooting have returned to work and are doing well. When I was asked to write about this incident, I had no second thoughts about it. I have a different outlook on life now and firmly believe we have an obligation to let our peers know we are there for them. A wellness program in every first-responder agency is absolutely essential; I'm living proof of it.

My training officer told me when I first started this job that I must always make sure to talk to family and friends, because otherwise this job would eat me alive. As first responders, we all see and hear things at work that no one should have to witness. The days of sucking it up and moving on have to come to an end. Look at it from this angle: If your wife or husband, brother or sister, daughter or son becomes sick, you take care of them.

As first responders, no matter what uniform or badge we wear, no matter what role we may play, we are all family. And we must always take care of each other and do whatever we can to emotionally survive and be well. We have it within our ability to save careers, marriages, and lives. There are so many positive steps we can take to care for ourselves and one another.

Struggling during the Aftermath

Tim and his wife, Elizabeth, struggled after his shooting, but as he explains, they tried to work their way through it. Things really became troublesome nearly two years later, when Tim was involved in an on-duty motorcycle collision. His wife was notified by the peer-support coordinator, and she met Tim at the hospital. The accident caused all of Elizabeth's previous emotional pain, fears, and anxieties to come to the surface — even more intensely than after the shooting.

Tim and Elizabeth began to have significant problems in their marriage. They were not talking much, and when they did talk they either remained distant or fought. In response, Tim became distant and emotionally withdrawn. Elizabeth kept trying to approach him, wanting to talk about their issues and what she was feeling inside, but she was met by the impenetrable wall that Tim had erected around himself. He did not realize how his wife was affected by his critical incidents, and what she was going through while trying to deal with the trauma in their marriage and her life. He eventually realized that his police job had seriously affected and damaged his wife's emotional well-being and sense of peace and security.

Both had to accept that these incidents were even harder for Elizabeth to deal with than for Tim. At least Tim could react at work, defend himself, fight, and have others come to his defense. But Elizabeth was on her own with few people to turn to — none of whom could understand what she was feeling inside. The serious fears, anxieties, and helpless feelings continued unabated and became harder for her to contain and deal with, while, at the same time, she did not want Tim to worry about her. Her emotions became debilitating for her and their marriage, and Tim, while becoming more isolated, distant, and disengaged, didn't respond in a way that was all that helpful.

Things would get worse before they improved. Tim was increasingly feeling helpless while still struggling with depression since his shooting. He was now beginning to lose hope, and he struggled for years. Here is Tim's account.

Restoring Hope

It's now been over seven years since my life was turned upside down because of my shooting, and a lot of things have changed during that time. I had continued working on my marriage and going to counseling, both with Elizabeth and without, and felt like I was making progress. The many deep scars left from what I experienced during the shooting, along with a motorcycle collision at work that caused a major concussion about two years later, were still with me every single day, but I felt like I had finally reached a point where I was normal again.

The discovery that I had been suffering from PTSD had been a huge breakthrough, and I finally felt like my old self again for the first time in over a year. However, after being back to work, I started to notice that my home life was still not the same. I could tell that something was still missing, even in deep conversation with Elizabeth; she seemed to be slipping away from our relationship. I firmly believed that I had done everything correct, that the department had stepped up and saved me, along with my home life, and we would finally be able to move on with the rest of our lives. I would soon learn that was not the case.

I began to feel like I just wasn't the husband she had married, and she began to distance herself. This didn't start immediately. I can say that looking back now, over all these years since I last wrote about this, that I missed so many red flags that Elizabeth had continued to raise. She had attempted many times to communicate with me. We spoke, but I completely missed the message she was sending. An example of this would be her asking me to go with her to watch the sunset on the beach or to do social activities, such as a baseball game with friends. I would always have an excuse to not do any of those things. I was isolating myself more and more, not realizing how it was affecting our marriage. I just wanted to stay in the house and have minimal contact with the outside world when I was not at work.

I remember several times thinking to myself that I should ask Elizabeth how I could be a better husband to her: "How can I help us become the couple we were before all this happened?" We were still going to counseling, at least I was going regularly, and I started to think that all of this would just work itself out. I believed our marriage together would continue for the rest of our lives and Elizabeth would always be there.

One Saturday morning, I could immediately tell something was wrong, and I can still see the look on Elizabeth's face as I approached her in the bedroom. She looked at me and said she no longer felt the same about our marriage. I asked her what she meant by that, and she simply stated, "I don't know if I love you anymore." I was absolutely floored and blindsided by this statement. My first reaction was to immediately pack up my things and leave the house. I turned completely defensive and felt extremely angry at her for saying that to me. My heart was broken instantly, for I had never loved someone as much as I loved her. I felt that I had failed her as a husband; and all the hard work, which I believed had successfully helped us, seemed pointless now. I had thought that we had healed our life, when in fact there was an infected wound that had festered — a wound that just would not heal, no matter how hard I tried to heal it on my own.

Shortly after Elizabeth shared those feelings with me, she decided she would stay with a friend for a few days to think about things. I did not want her to go, and we agreed that we would talk about things, return to counseling, and not rush into a separation. She did come home after a few days, and we continued to struggle.

I immediately made an appointment with our counselor, and during that first session it was determined that I needed to address a few things. I was still extremely depressed and realized I had been ever since my shooting three years ago. With Elizabeth now saying that she may not love me anymore, I really began to relapse and lost all control over my emotions. I was full of anger, deep depression, and a terrible feeling of helplessness and hopelessness. I couldn't get to sleep at night because Elizabeth was not coming home by midnight, immediately after work, like she usually did. Some nights it would be 3 or 4 AM before she got home. This went on for about three months, and the communication between us ceased. I was progressively falling into an even deeper depression. My head was an absolute mess, and I couldn't find meaning in my life anymore. Elizabeth was my meaning in life, and without her nothing else made any sense.

It was the day after Christmas, 2013, when I received a text message from Elizabeth. The message stated that she would not be at the house when I came home from work and that she would be going once again to stay with a friend for a few days. That moment hit me harder than anything I have ever experienced. It physically took my breath away. I called her to beg her not to leave. I would have done anything at that point to stop her, but she would not answer my calls.

I resorted to doing what I always did. I continued to work my shift while trying to remain focused on work, but I became extremely angry and very sad at the same time over what had happened. Once my shift ended, I could not get home fast enough. I pulled into the driveway and immediately noticed that our home looked different. Elizabeth's car was gone. All the lights inside were turned off, and I knew she was gone from my life. I knew that she probably would never come back, and that was a terrible feeling of despair that nearly sent me over the edge.

I walked into the darkened house and heard complete silence. To this day, it was one of the most heartbreaking moments in my life. I felt something that I could never describe to anyone other than as complete sadness, despair, emptiness inside. I felt physically ill. After walking into every room, looking at everything in the house that Elizabeth and I had built together, I fell down onto my knees and cried for hours. It was one of the most terrifying things that I have ever experienced. I could not think, speak, or put anything together in my mind, except I knew I had people who I could reach out to. People who I knew would be there for me because they had helped me during the shooting, the aftermath of dealing with the guilt of taking those children's father, and the motorcycle collision.

Though I had thought of suicide during my many struggles after my shooting, such hopeless thoughts were now suddenly even more intense. This was the worst moment in my life as I sat in despair with thoughts of killing myself. Yet I knew that would have hurt everyone who cared for me. Instead I managed to pull myself up and make that phone call. Because of my department's peer-support team, my life was saved again. I had *someone there with me twenty minutes after I made that call. I thank them every day for being there for me and helping me get through that terrible night. They saved my life.*

Weeks slowly turned into months, and Elizabeth never came back home. We talked about once a week, but I knew the marriage was over. I knew that she was hurting inside as well, and I made several attempts to help her get into counseling. She never accepted it. The long nightmare of the inevitable divorce shattered me, but I always had friends from work who showed me all the time how much they cared for and supported me.

I struggled, but I sought help, which saved me. I kept focusing on trying to do the next right thing, each day, each moment to just get me through another day.

The department was able to send me to the West Coast Post-trauma Retreat [WCPR, 415-721-9789, www.frsn.org /retreats/wcpr], a treatment facility in Northern California specifically for police and all other first responders, including corrections officers. [There is a similar treatment facility in Maryland specifically for firefighters: IAFF Center of Excellence for Behavioral Health Treatment and Recovery, 855-900-8437, www.iaffrecoverycenter.com. The International Association of Fire Fighters plans to establish one on the West Coast and in the Midwest as well.]

To this day, that retreat was one of the best gifts I have ever been given. The WCPR is a safe six-day residential treatment center where you attend with other first responders who are suffering from PTSD, as well as possibly addictions and other issues resulting from our trauma experiences. It was an incredible, lifesaving experience because I was introduced to the extremely effective PTSD treatment called EMDR.

EMDR helped me to finally heal from my PTSD, which had plagued me for over three years. It helped me to get unstuck, to disassociate myself from all the horrible thoughts and emotions attached to my trauma experience memories, so that I could once again be normal and have my mind function properly. It enabled me to file away in my mind a lot of things and to put them into their proper perspective so that they no longer crippled me. I didn't forget the memories, but with EMDR I can now think about them and talk about them without suffering any negative or debilitating effects.

Finally, over a year and a half later, I was fully back to loving my life again. I could never have made it without the people who cared and helped me. The department's peer-support team and our police psychologist saved me, and I was once again able to stand up and love the amazing thing we call life.

After about two years, I decided to date again. I found the woman who I truly believe is my soul mate. We were married in July of 2016. I can't express how much I love her and our life now. I am so happy being married to my best friend who understands me, loves me, and is always there.

I have learned also just how important it is to never take anything for granted in this world. But the most important thing I now know is that without good, caring people who will stop and offer emotional support for someone in a time of hurt or loss, the world would have many more terrible tragedies, suicides, and desperate people. I am living proof of that.

You can heal from trauma with treatments such as EMDR. You do not have to suffer endlessly. PTSD does not just go away with time unless you do something helpful. Reach out, get help, and find ways to regain your life. There was that time when I thought it impossible for life to get better. I love life now more than ever; so can you.

CONCLUSION

A career as a first responder involves sacrifice, a giving of oneself, and a selfless devotion to protect and give life to others. Inherent in these noble professions is a continual assault upon your spirit. Combating the evil actions of others while trying not to suffer with your victims makes it a daily struggle to emotionally survive.

The message of this book is one of hope and promise. It is not inevitable that you will suffer and become a victim of your profession. First responders are not victims — but survivors and warriors of spirit. The emotional- and spiritual-wellness principles that you have learned in this book can enable you not only to emotionally survive but to thrive throughout your career while positively affecting countless lives. It is imperative that you take the wellness of your spirit seriously, while working to protect, nurture, and sustain your soul. The protection of your community, the quality of your personal and professional life, the happiness of your family, and the wellness of your spirit all depend upon it.

There is honor in the work you do. Practice taking better care of yourself and those who serve by your side. By working together to promote emotional survival, we can all sustain wellness while protecting those who depend upon us for their life and well-being. Always remember the tremendous healing capacity of your heart. Be driven by your heart to serve with compassion to make a positive difference within your agency, with your colleagues, within the community, and for those you serve. May you experience all the peace, joy, purpose, and fulfillment that a noble life of service has to offer.

ACKNOWLEDGMENTS

As I contemplate all the people to whom I am forever grateful, I realize that all of what we are, and most of what we have ever done, is the result of the influence of others. My greatest wish is to pass forward the good that I have received and to become a positive influence on others in order to help them heal, to serve to protect and enrich their spirits, and to carry on the fight of good against evil in protecting life.

I am first and foremost grateful to acknowledge all those emergency first responders who have come before me, whose sacrifices and selfless service I owe my life to. I will forever be thankful to La Mesa police lieutenant Carl Wirtz, whose kind and compassionate guidance saved my law-enforcement career just as it was starting. I am grateful to all my police academy instructors, my supervisors, my mentors, my field training officers, and my colleagues, who not only taught me but also inspired me throughout my career.

I also acknowledge Sam Feemster, a supervising special agent with the FBI (now retired), who kindled my passion to work to bring about the emotional survival and healing of our heroes' minds, bodies, and spirits.

I am grateful for my literary agent, Claire Gerus; my editor, Julie McCarron; and my publisher, Georgia Hughes of New World Library, all of whom helped give life to an idea and simple words that will give hope and life to others.

I will forever be grateful to those who taught me the eternal importance and value of one's spirit, the Reverend Flower A. Newhouse and the Reverend Stephen Isaac. They inspired a young boy to develop, nurture, and sustain the spirit within and make life meaningful by loving and serving others.

Of course, I also acknowledge my parents, particularly my beloved mother. My parents taught me the meaning of selfless sacrifice, hard work, and compassion every day of their lives. When I was a young boy, my mother used to read me bedtime stories about great people in history. She would always tell me that life was a precious gift from God and that I had a solemn responsibility to make something out of my life by doing good and serving others. It is she who inspired me to become a police officer in order to protect and give life to others.

Finally, I acknowledge the kindness, caring, and love of many others whose goodness has served to heal my heart, comfort my soul, and breathe life into my spirit. Every experience is meant to be a teacher, one that hopefully teaches the lessons of love. I'm grateful for every person and experience that has increased my heart's capacity to love, to serve, and to make a positive difference.

WELLNESS PROGRAM SURVEY

In order for a wellness program to become effective and promote employee buy-in and interest throughout the agency, all employees' input must be solicited. The most effective wellness initiatives, however, are ideas from frontline employees. This anonymous survey can be used by any agency that is initiating a wellness program or that wants to gauge the effectiveness of its current wellness program.

1. How long have you been an emergency first responder?
   a. 0–5 years
   b. 6–10 years
   c. 11–20 years
   d. 21+ years

2. Are you a sworn or a nonsworn employee?

3. What was the primary reason you wanted a career as an emergency first responder?

4. Do you feel that the job currently fulfills that goal?

   Yes   No

   Why or why not?

5. Do you believe the job has adversely affected you, your outlook on life, your emotional wellness, or your relationships away from work?

   Yes   No

   If yes, in what way(s)?

6. Has your family or someone else close to you told you that you have changed since you began your emergency-first-responder career?

   Yes   No

   If yes, in what way(s)?

7. Name any specific issues or circumstances related to your job that adversely affect your general wellness.

8. List any specific habits, hobbies, or interests that you enjoyed and regularly participated in before you began your emergency-first-responder career, and that you either no longer enjoy or no longer participate in to the same level.

9. What coping mechanisms, if any, do you regularly rely on to deal with stress and issues from work?

   a. None
   b. Exercise / group sports
   c. Vacation / time off
   d. Meditation
   e. Faith-based activities
   f. Hobbies
   g. Self-medication (alcohol or drugs)
   h. Spending time with family
   i. Counseling
   j. Talking with friends
   k. Gambling
   l. Promiscuity or other reckless or dangerous behavior
   m. Shopping / buying things
   n. Extreme sports or other high-risk activities
   o. Other (please describe):

10. Which personal issues listed below directly impact you, those close to you, or your job performance?

    a. Finances/bankruptcy/foreclosure
    b. Divorce
    c. Troubled relationships
    d. Depression
    e. Suicidal thoughts (current or formerly)
    f. Alcohol
    g. Prescription medications
    h. Anger
    i. Sleep deprivation / sleep problems
    j. Domestic violence

    k.   Organizational stress from the agency/command staff/supervisors

    l.   PTSD / issues related to a critical incident(s) at work

    m.   Other (please list):

11. How much does the agency promote or train individuals in emotional-survival and wellness issues?

    a.   Not at all

    b.   Very little

    c.   Very little, and I would like to see more

    d.   Moderate level

    e.   Moderate level, and I would like to see more

    f.   High level

    g.   High level, and I would like to see more

    h.   Too much

12. Is there emotional-survival/wellness training you would like to see?

Yes   No

Please list any training you would like to see.

ENDNOTES

Introduction

Page 1 *on average about 120 to 140 documented yearly:* Christal Hayes, "'Silence Can Be Deadly': 46 Officers Were Fatally Shot Last Year. More Than Triple That — 140 — Committed Suicide," *USA Today*, April 11, 2018, https://www.usatoday.com/story/news/2018/04/11/ officers-firefighters-suicides-study/503735002/. These numbers also reflect those reported in the ongoing research of John M. Violanti, PhD, author of *Police Suicide: Epidemic in Blue* (Springfield, IL: Charles C. Thomas, 2007).

Page 2 *On average, one active-duty soldier and 21 veterans:* Melanie Haiken, "Suicide Rate among Vets and Active Duty Military Jumps — Now 22 a Day," Forbes.com, February 5, 2013, www.forbes.com/sites /melaniehaiken/2013/02/05/22-the-number-of-veterans-who-now -commit-suicide-every-day.

Page 2 *some estimates showing PTSD rates:* Terry Spencer, "PTSD and Suicide in the U.S. Fire Service," December 10, 2016, Firefighter Nation, https://www.firefighternation.com/articles/2016/12/ptsd -and-suicide-in-the-u-s-fire-service.html.

Page 2 *25 to 30 percent of police officers have stress-based physical health problems:* Janice Wood, "Stress Creates Significant Health, Mental Risks for Police," Psychcentral.com, July 12, 2012, http://psychcentral .com/news/2012/07/12/stress-creates-significant-health-mental -risks-for-police/41451.html.

Page 2 *A 2007 research study by Harvard Medical School:* Shantha M.W. Rajaratnam et al., "Sleep Disorders, Health, and Safety in Police Officers," *Journal of the American Medical Association* 306 no. 23 (December 21, 2011), http://jama.jamanetwork.com/article.aspx?articleid=1104746.

Chapter One. The Warning Signs and Self-Awareness

Page 15 *Alcohol abuse among US police officers:* Elizabeth A. Willman, "Alcohol Use among Law Enforcement," *Journal of Law Enforcement* 2, no. 3 (2012), www.jghcs.info/index.php/l/article/view/150.

Page 16 *39 percent of veterans screened positive:* Join Together staff, "Active-Duty Military and Veterans Prone to Substance Abuse, Depression, and Suicide," Drugfree.org, January 26, 2012, www.drugfree.org/join-together/alcohol/active-duty-military-and-veterans-prone-to-substance-abuse-depression-and-suicide.

Page 16 *29 percent of active-duty firefighters:* International Association of Fire Fighters, "Alcohol and Drug Use, Abuse and Dependence," undated, www.iaff.org/ET/JobAid/EAP/Drug_and_Alcohol_Use.htm (accessed May 24, 2014).

Page 16 *the chances of killing yourself increase tenfold:* John M. Violanti, PhD, "Predictors of Police Suicide Ideation," *Suicide and Life Threatening Behavior* 34, no. 3 (fall 2004): 277–83, https://www.ncbi.nlm.nih.gov/pubmed/15385182.

Page 16 *At least 20 percent of first responders will experience:* Indra Cidambi, MD, "Police and Addiction," *Psychology Today*, March 30, 2018, https://www.psychologytoday.com/us/blog/sure-recovery/201803/police-and-addiction.

Chapter Two. Spiritual Wellness

Page 28 *Consistent exercise will reduce by 58 percent:* Sheri R. Colberg et al., "Exercise and Type 2 Diabetes," American Diabetes Association, *Diabetes Care* 33, no. 12 (December 2010), http://care.diabetesjournals.org/content/33/12/e147.full.

Page 39   *Science has shown that meditating for just a few minutes:*
National Institutes of Health: National Center for Complementary
and Integrative Health, "Meditation: In Depth," April 2016,
https://nccih.nih.gov/health/meditation/overview.htm.

Page 39   *Yale University has developed a course:* David Shimer,
"Yale's Most Popular Class Ever: Happiness," January 26, 2018,
https://www.nytimes.com/2018/01/26/nyregion/at-yale-class-on
-happiness-draws-huge-crowd-laurie-santos.html; and A.
Pawlowski, "Yale's Most Popular Class Teaches Happiness: 6
Lessons You Can Practice Now," TODAY.com, February 19, 2018,
https://www.today.com/health/yale-popular-happiness-class-6
-lessons-you-can-practice-now-t123226.

Chapter Three. Emotional Wellness

Page 50   *The study showed that officers with sleep disorders:* Shantha
M. W. Rajaratnam et al., "Sleep Disorders, Health, and Safety in
Police Officers," *Journal of the American Medical Association* 306
no. 23 (December 21, 2011), http://jama.jamanetwork.com/article
.aspx?articleid=1104746.

Page 54   *Listening to music, especially slow, quiet classical music:*
Jane Collingwood, "The Power of Music to Reduce Stress,"
Psychcentral.com, October 8, 2018, http://psychcentral.com
/lib/the-power-of-music-to-reduce-stress/000930.

Chapter Six. The Spirituality of Service

Page 100   *"People must open themselves to the idea…":* Stephan A.
Schwartz, "The Matrix of Life with Stephan A. Schwartz:
New Thinking Allowed with Jeffrey Mishlove," May 24, 2017,
https://www.youtube.com/watch?v=hPsh1GZfTGo.

Page 109   *"The best and most beautiful things in the world…":* Helen
Keller, *The Story of My Life* (New York: Doubleday, Page & Co.,
1903), 203.

RESOURCES

Books

Blum, Lawrence. *Force under Pressure: How Cops Live and Why They Die*. Lantern Books, 2000.

DeCarvalho, Lorie, and Julia Whealin. *Healing Stress in Military Families: Eight Steps to Wellness*. Wiley, 2012.

Gilmartin, Kevin M. *Emotional Survival for Law Enforcement: A Guide for Officers and Their Families*. E-S Press, 2002. You may contact the author at email ghakev@aol.com. Gilmartin travels throughout the country giving lectures on emotional survival to emergency first responders.

Grossman, David, and Loren Christensen. *On Combat: The Psychology and Physiology of Deadly Conflict in War and in Peace*. Warrior Science Publications, 2008. Also, Grossman, David, Michael Asken, and Loren Christensen. *Warrior Mindset: Mental Toughness Skills for a Nation's Peacekeepers*. Human Factor Research Group, 2012. Lt. Col. David Grossman lectures throughout the nation on mental preparedness and emotional survival for emergency first responders. His website is www.killology.com, and he can be contacted at info@killology.com or by calling 618-566-4682.

Ingemann, Mira. *NeXus: Firefighter Wellness Program*. Regent University Press, 2007.

Kirschman, Ellen. *I Love a Cop: What Police Families Need to Know*. Guilford Press, 2006.

Paris, Clarke. *My Life for Your Life*. Pain Behind the Badge, 2011. The author travels throughout the country lecturing on police suicide. His website is http://thepain behindthebadge.com, and he can be contacted at training@thepainbehindthebadge.com or by calling 702-573-4263.

Shapiro, Francine. *Getting Past Your Past: Take Control of Your Life with Self-Help Techniques from EMDR Therapy*. Rodale, 2013.

Smith, Bobby. *Visions of Courage: The Bobby Smith Story*. Four Winds Publishing, 2000. Retired Louisiana state trooper Bobby Smith is also the author of *The Will to Survive* (Visions of Courage Publishing, 2005) and *What's in Your Heart Comes out of Your Mouth* (Visions of Courage Publishing, 2013). He lectures throughout the nation on emotional survival. Bobby's website is http://visionsofcourage.com, and he can be contacted at bobbysmith@visionsofcourage.com.

van der Kolk, Bessel. *The Body Keeps the Score: Brain, Mind, and Body in the Healing of Trauma*. Penguin Books, 2015.

Websites and Other Sources

American Addiction Centers, https://americanaddiction centers.org/firefighters-first-responders. Addiction resources for any first responder.

Blue Courage, http://bluecourage.com. Offers excellent training and other resources for police.

The Code Green Campaign, http://codegreencampaign.org
/resources. Offers an extensive list of resources in every
state.

Code 9: Officer Needs Assistance. This is a great short docu-
mentary highlighting PTSD among police officers,
www.youtube.com/watch?v=PapXcCACSwc (Dangerous
Curves Productions, uploaded on February 26, 2012).

CopsAlive, www.copsalive.com. This site was founded by the
Law Enforcement Survival Institute to provide information and strategies to help police officers and agencies
successfully survive their careers and prepare for the
risks that threaten their existence.

Counseling Team International, http://thecounselingteam
.com. Nancy Bohl-Penrod, PhD, is an emergency-first-
responder trauma expert and can be reached at
cteamnbohl@aol.com.

Courage to Call. Free 24/7 helpline entirely staffed by veterans who have recently served in the military. They provide information, guidance, support, and/or referrals to
current and former members of the military, reserves, or
National Guard, and their families and loved ones. They
can be reached at 211, 1-877-MyUSVet, or 1-877-698-7838.

1st Responder Conferences, https://1stresponderconferences.org.
Provides wellness training throughout the country.

First Responder Support Network, 415-721-9789, http://www
.frsn.org. Their mission is to provide treatment programs that promote recovery from stress and critical
incidents for first responders and their families.

In Harm's Way: Law Enforcement Suicide Prevention,
http://policesuicide.spcollege.edu. Offers training seminars and workshops on suicide prevention. The webpage

supplies resources, reproducible materials, articles with varying viewpoints, statistics, and opinions from which readers can form their own conclusions on the magnitude of the law-enforcement suicide problem, its causes, and the best approaches to finding a solution. The seminars and workshops are offered through a partnership of the Florida Regional Community Policing Institute at St. Petersburg College; The United States Attorney's Office, Middle District of Florida; and the Survivors of Law Enforcement Suicides (SOLES).

Institute for Responder Wellness, https://instituteforresponder wellness.com.

International Association of Chiefs of Police, www.theiacp.org /resources/document/law-enforcement-suicide-prevention -and-awareness. The International Association of Chiefs of Police and the United States Department of Justice have partnered to produce a compilation of suicide-prevention resources from leading agencies across the nation. This site provides information on how to develop suicide-prevention programs and the ways to implement them; brochures, posters, and program summaries; numerous sample training materials; several sample presentations covering prevention, intervention, and other topics; and sample funeral protocols for officer suicides.

International Association of Fire Fighters Center of Excellence for Behavioral Health Treatment and Recovery, www.iaff recoverycenter.com. Based in Maryland and working on opening treatment centers on the West Coast and in the Midwest. Offers all treatments for trauma, PTSD, addictions, and any other issues for firefighters.

National Fallen Firefighters Foundation, www.firehero.org. This organization has launched a major initiative to reduce firefighter deaths.

National Law Enforcement Cancer Support Foundation,
   http://lawenforcementcancer.org. Operated by police
   officer cancer survivors, this organization offers support and assistance to fellow law-enforcement officers
   struggling with cancer. The organization can be reached
   at 888-456-5327.

National Police Suicide Foundation, www.psf.org. This organization was founded by retired Baltimore police officer
   Robert Douglas, who now lectures throughout the
   country and in other nations regarding first-responder
   suicide awareness and prevention and emotional survival. He can be contacted at redoug2001@aol.com or
   866-276-4615.

National Suicide Prevention Lifeline, http://suicideprevention
   lifeline.org. Addresses traumatic brain injury, including
   PTSD; suicide prevention; and other crises. You can talk
   to a trained Veterans Administration professional at no
   cost, twenty-four hours a day, seven days a week, regarding
   crisis counseling, suicide intervention, thoughts of harming
   someone else, and mental health referral information. Call
   800-273-TALK (8255); press #1 if you're a veteran.

Promises Behavioral Health, https://www.promisesbehavioral
   health.com/treatment/first-responders-trauma-treatment.
   Help and assistance for first responders.

Reviving Responders, www.revivingresponders.com/needhelp
   now. Excellent resources.

Safe Call Now, www.safecallnow.org. This organization is
   a confidential resource for public-safety employees,
   including law enforcement, firefighters, and other first
   responders, as well as for corrections staff and civilian
   support staff and their families.

Spirituality Activated Law Enforcement Training, www.911salt
   .com. This website is operated by Samuel Feemster (a

supervising special agent with the FBI, now retired, who worked with the Behavioral Science Unit). Feemster has conducted years of research into the emotional harm that is done to those in the law-enforcement profession. He is available to travel to any agency for training regarding issues of emotional survival.

Stress Center at UC Health, Dr. Kate Chard, PhD, University of Cincinnati, Psychiatry and Behavioral Neuroscience. https://uchealth.com/stress-center, 513-861-3100.

INDEX

addictions, 1, 16, 73, 119. *See also* alcohol abuse; substance abuse
administrative leave, 215
Afghanistan, 191
aging, premature, 2
alarm, 118
Albuquerque (NM), 97–99
alcohol abuse, 29; depression and, 92; family and, 86; hypervigilance and, 46, 52; PTSD and, 16, 52, 73, 93, 118–19, 124; reduction of, 31, 51, 52; self-awareness questions, 40; sleep disorders and, 51; as soporific, 40, 43; support services for, 92–93; as warning sign, 15–16, 178
Alcoholics Anonymous, 166
alcoholism, 95
Alicia (firefighter's wife), 175–76
altruism, 27
ambition, unbridled, 109
American Addiction Centers, 242
American Medical Association (AMA), 2
American Psychiatric Association, 125
amygdala, 71

anger: as first-responder hazard, 2, 190; letting go of, 35, 37, 48; negative effects of, 106–7, 110; as PTSD symptom, 75–76, 118, 124; relaxation techniques for reducing, 53–54; sleep disorders and, 50; as warning sign, 14, 15
anxiety: compassionate service and reduction of, 105; as first-responder hazard, 2; as PTSD symptom, 11, 69, 72, 118, 124; as warning sign, 15
apathy, 14–15, 45, 47, 48, 110. *See also* disengagement; emotional distancing
Aristotle, 135
arrests, 104, 111, 202
Asken, Michael, 241

Baker to Vegas Challenge, 152
Basu, Moni, 191
BeSTOW (Beyond Survival Toward Officer Wellness) philosophy: benefits of, 7; challenges to, 151; community involvement in, 151–53;

ABOUT THE AUTHOR

Captain Dan Willis (ret.) is an international instructor in trauma, post-traumatic stress, and the process of healing with the International Academy of Public Safety. The founder of www.first responderwellness.com, he provides wellness training to first-responder agencies throughout North America. For nearly thirty years, Captain Willis served as a police officer for the La Mesa Police Department near San Diego, California. He was a homicide detective for nine years, investigating crimes of violence and cold cases; a SWAT commander; and the developer and coordinator of the police department's wellness program. He graduated from San Diego State University with a bachelor of science degree in criminal justice, and graduated from the FBI's National Academy for senior police managers in Quantico, Virginia, where he studied emotional survival, trauma, and the process of healing.

Captain Willis was La Mesa's Officer of the Year twice within four years, was nominated as Detective of the Year for the State of California, and was nominated as Homicide Detective of the Year by the California Homicide Investigators Association.

For twelve years, Captain Willis was an instructor for the San Diego Public Safety Institute, the county's police academy. He now travels throughout the United States and Canada providing training to any first-responder agency regarding trauma, PTSD, the process of healing, and emotional survival. At the time of this writing, he has given over two hundred presentations in twenty-eight states and Canada. He lives in San Diego, California.

His website is www.firstresponderwellness.com, or contact him via email at dwillis1121@yahoo.com.

TRAINING AND SEMINAR INFORMATION

Captain Willis (ret.) is available to travel to any location to present a training session on trauma, PTSD, the process of healing, and emotional survival as well as on the book *Bulletproof Spirit*. Requests for training and information can be sent to Captain Dan Willis at dwillis1121@yahoo.com or www.firstresponderwellness.com.

Captain Willis makes available upon request numerous training bulletins on various issues: *Emotional and Spiritual Wellness*; *Emotional Survival Practices*; *Managing the Hypervigilance Cycle*; *How Your Family Can Support You*; *Nobility of Police Service*; *Preparing for PTSD and Acute Stress*; *Promoting Emotional-Spiritual Wellness among Ourselves*; *Spirituality in Law Enforcement as a Shield*; *Stress*; *Stress Management*; *Stress Prevention and Processing*; *Suicide Prevention and Awareness*; *Supporting Officers after a Critical Incident*; *EMDR*; and *Combat-Tactical Breathing*. There are also several BeSTOW emotional-wellness quarterly newsletters available. In addition, our department instructions for our Wellness Program (regarding peer support and the BeSTOW philosophy) and our Chaplain Program's standard operating procedures are available upon request.

Emergency-first-responder agencies may receive any training materials or information on the La Mesa Police Department Wellness Program and the BeSTOW training philosophy from Captain Dan Willis at dwillis1121@yahoo.com.